IN
PURSUIT
OF
Surrender

IN PURSUIT OF
Surrender

Angelique A. Strothers

Cover Design: Soleil Branding Essentials
Internal Layout: InSCRIBEd Inspiration, LLC.

ISBN Number: Paperback: 978-1-7357407-0-6
E-book (Kindle): 978-1-7357407-1-3

Dedication

"For those who don't know me, this may seem odd or even a little narcissistic; but at the risk of seeming vain, I dedicate this book to myself. This book is the culmination of 34 years of my lived experience and what God's been teaching me through it all. The one thing that He's still teaching me heavily in this season of my life is how to LOVE myself. With that in mind, I'm not sending me flowers or chocolates. My primary love language is Words of Affirmation, so:

To, Angelique Antoinette Strothers,

You are so worthy of love, attention, affection, and every good thing you've ever desired. Honey, you are fierce! You are an untamable fire! You are formidable! You are unbelievably anointed. You are chosen! You defy categorization! You are not one thing; you are a multitude! You are beautiful! You are gorgeous and you are worthy of celebration!

May every part of this book be a celebration of the journey you've taken thus far, the woman you've become and all that is yet to come. Let every paragraph, every line, every word and every letter of this tome remind you of who you are in Christ. Woman... Lady... Queen, I love you more today than every day before. May God teach me to love you infinitely more.

Love,
Yourself

Amended February 2021 in honor of my Mother:

To, My Dear, Sweet Mama,

*You graduated just months before getting to see this dream – this prophesied promise – come to fruition. But, I will always carry with me the way you've loved and supported me on this and every journey I've walked in this life. Although I wish that you were still here on this side of Heaven to see the manifestation of so many of the prayers you've prayed for me, I am encouraged to know that you have now joined that great cloud of witnesses and you are cheering me on to the finish line. In my spirit's eye, I can see you smiling that smile that lit up every room you entered. That smile of pride that comes when a mother sees that her child "gets it." Mom, for all the nights you stayed awake interceding for us, for all the tears you cried along the way, for every moment of triumph and trial, **this** moment is for you. I "get it" and I am forever grateful that you chose to instill "it" in us from the time that we were born. Thank you, Mommy. This one's for you.*

With So Much Love,
Your Spider Legs, a.k.a. Your Quiet Child,
Angelique Antoinette Strothers

I will stand at my watch and station myself on the ramparts;
I will look to see what he will say to me, and what answer I
am to give to this complaint.
Habakkuk 2:1 NIV

Foreword

Ladies and Gentlemen,

You have been warned (pun intended)!
Your eyes are about to read the words of what I have personally witnessed, a surrendered life. It has been at least seven years since we sat in our small group, both quiet, both introverts, suffering through Icebreakers (an introvert's favorite thing to participate in), but both growing. Growing in Christ, but also growing in relationship with one another. We went from small group members, to accountability partners, to an all-encompassing sisterhood. You name it, we be it, at any given time!

Angelique has morphed from a Watchman on the wall waiting patiently for God's promises to be fulfilled in her life to a Watchman who stands guard, watches, and warns. Whether she is unapologetically offering a prophetic word or inviting you into worship with her and her Baba, Sis is a force to be reckoned with for God's glory.

And now, because she has positioned herself to hear from God and because she has surrendered to the wait time, we have this beautiful baby named, IPoS (please do not give this name to your children, instill it in them, but I beg of you, no IPoS on school roster). You will be blessed by this unselfish gift, that shares the journey, while on the journey.

> "So, I have spent the last several years listening for His voice and taking notes. I've received the words that He's spoken to me, I've prayed over them, I've prayed about what part He wants me to play in bringing His word to pass, if any."

In Pursuit of Surrender (IPoS), Chapter 4 Surrendering To Perfect Love: Watchmen – Angelique A. Strothers

This book, my friend, is the power of surrender. You have been warned.

Amy L. Boyd, Author
"Like A Tree Planted By the Water"

IN
PURSUIT
OF
Surrender

Contents

1. Surrendering Rejection 1

2. Surrendering In The Midst Of Pain 19

3. Surrendering My Mind 21

4. Surrendering To Perfect Love 27

5. Surrendering My Excuses 35

6. Surrendering In The Fight 47

7. Surrendering In The Wait 55

8. Surrendering To Shedding 59

9. Surrendering To Selective Memory 65

10. Surrendering My Fallacy 73

11. Surrendering My Plans 79

12. Surrendering The Weight 85

13. Surrendering Impatience 89

14. Surrendering In My Singlehood 97

15. Surrendering My Brokenness, Part 1 111

16. Surrendering My Brokenness, Part 2 115

17. Surrendering My Brokenness, Part 3 121

18. Surrendering The Need For Significance 129

19. Surrendering Timidity 135

20. Surrendering My Biology 147

21. Surrendering Procrastination 163

22. Surrendering My Emotions 171

23. Surrendering Comparison, Pt. 1 179

24. Surrendering Comparison, Pt. 2 189

25. Surrendering My Desires 199

26. Surrendering Hurt Feelings 203

27. Surrendering My Wounds 213

28. Surrendering "Them" 231

29. Surrendering Pride 237

30. Surrendering My "Not Enough" 245

Prologue

"Not that I have already obtained all this, or have already arrived at my goal, but I press on to take hold of that for which Christ Jesus took hold of me. Brothers and sisters, I do not consider myself yet to have taken hold of it. But one thing I do: Forgetting what is behind and straining toward what is ahead, I press on toward the goal to win the prize for which God has called me heavenward in Christ Jesus."

> *"Surrender is a moment to moment, second to second decision."*

Clearly, these are not my words. They are the words of the Apostle Paul found in Philippians 3:12-14 (NIV) . However, though they are not my own, they do communicate my heart in sharing this book with you. Surrender is not something that I've already obtained; it doesn't happen overnight, and it's not a place at which you can "arrive." It is a daily journey that continues until the day you die. Surrender is a daily choice, and indeed a series of choices each day.

Surrender is a moment to moment, second to second decision; and if you are, even for a second, not intentional about it, you could find yourself slipping back into the cockpit of your own life, fighting for control again. This book is not meant to be a one-and-done, be-all-end-all, guaranteed surrender guide. This is not an "As Seen On TV," or "Get your life together in three easy steps," type of deal. I've included the dates on which most entries were written because I wanted you to see the process of surrender in real time. Don't let the dates confuse you, they are only there to provide a chronological frame of reference.

This book simply chronicles my journey of surrender thus far, my reflections and God's revelation while in the process and in retrospect. That's why this book is called *In Pursuit of Surrender* and not How to Surrender: A Quick & Easy Guide, because I will be pursuing surrender unto God until the day I die and see Him face to face. Also, there is no "quick & easy" way to surrender. Inherently, surrender is difficult, and even messy, sometimes. Surrender requires one party deferring to another, giving control to another, relinquishing authority to another. As you can imagine, for one party that has been in control of their own trajectory for some time, it is a difficult task to give up all claims to the control to which they've become accustomed.

This book is meant to give you a vulnerable glimpse at some of the places where God has had to teach me the hard lessons of surrender. I am intensely transparent here about my struggles and experiences because I know that we overcome by the blood of The Lamb and the word of our testimony; and I want you to overcome. We all need to know that we are not alone in our struggles; someone else has overcome them before; someone else is going through the same thing. 1 Peter 5:9 tells us to, "Resist him [the devil], standing firm in the faith, because you know that the family of believers throughout the world is undergoing the same kind of sufferings." This book is just a look into some of the most intimate struggles we share and the revelation that God has been sharing with me to teach me how to overcome.

You will not find magic formulas between the covers of this book. It's not intended to function as a checklist; it is meant to provide a starting point on your journey of surrender to God, to challenge you to surrender more, to surrender all. My hope is that when you get to see my vulnerability in sharing some of the struggles I've gone through, and sometimes still fight through, you will be freed to be vulnerable before God and an accountability partner or group because, make no mistake, you cannot be free if you are not honest with yourself, God and your point(s) of accountability. The primary tools that we're putting to work here are God-guided introspection, God-breathed scripture and fervent prayer.

I strongly encourage you to get a journal, even if you're not normally a journaler. My recommendation is the *In Pursuit of Surrender Journal* which is specifically made to coincide with your reading of this book. The journal includes the reflection questions, activities, free space to write your own prayers of surrender to God and so much more. Here are a few advantages to using a journal:

- You can go back and see your growth,
- You can go back and be reminded of your prayers and what you are still trusting God to answer,
- You can write out the truth of your experience so that after a chapter of your life has been surrendered you have a written record of God's power, work and faithfulness,
- You can write down your expectations for deliverance on your surrender journey and check 'em off as God does what He does best, and finally,
- It's often easier to write some things than to say them out loud. I recognize within my own journey that sometimes it was hard for me to pray over certain areas of my life out loud. It was difficult to hear those things about myself. So, I started by praying them in a prayer journal first before I could verbalize them to God and myself.

Bear in mind that while this book is meant to be an "easy read" linguistically, if not contextually, don't rush through. You'll see that many chapters have exercises attached to them; take your time working through each chapter and exercise. You may find that, while focusing on a particular chapter exercise, you want to go back and re-read a chapter. Maybe you were particularly challenged by a chapter and you want to hover there a while before moving to the next chapter. That's okay!

Some chapters have specific reflection questions or prayer foci. In these chapters, I've listed one or two foci or questions there for you; however, you can find the full list of prayer foci and reflection questions in the *IPoS Journal*. Now, not every chapter has reflection questions, a follow-up or activity attached to it, that doesn't mean that God isn't going to challenge you in those chapters too. Perhaps, instead of following a carefully thought out exercise, God wants you to seek Him directly for guidance to determine what to do with the information you encountered in that chapter. Don't breeze past those chapters and don't be limited by the exercises in the book. Always listen for His voice. How is He leading you? Maybe He wants you to extend an exercise so that it becomes a habit for you. Let His voice be the loudest one you hear.

Feel free to take your time and work through, not just this book, but your life. I would rather you read one chapter a week for thirty weeks (just as an example) and really apply the principles to your life than to read one chapter a day for thirty days and get nothing substantive. Ultimately, I pray that by the time you finish this book you will be certain of three fundamental truths:

- You are not alone.
- You can be free from things that bind you, but,
- Your freedom will only come through your surrender to God.

In Pursuit of Surrender,
Angelique A. Strothers

"Though He slay me…"
~Job

Surrendering Rejection
(2/11/2017)

"If you want different results you've gotta do something different." So, I did. I did it! I stepped way outside of my comfort zone and auditioned. Previously, I had been too afraid to put myself out there; but, this time, I auditioned! I was called back for a second audition and the casting team said they were pleased. Fast forward about a month and a half to now; it is one week before rehearsals begin and not so much as an e-mail saying, "yes" or "no". Other cast members are now sharing the news that they've been cast so… I guess that's my answer.

But, it doesn't make sense! I did something different! You told me to stop hiding; I finally stopped hiding and still got the same result?! Wasn't this supposed to be the triumphant part of the movie when the music swells and the guy gets the girl and the whale leaps the barrier and the prince saves the princess and the girl lands the role?! What the ham & crackers?! Where's my music swell?! Where's my prince and my whale and my role?! What kind of movie is this?!

". . . I've got nothing left to give God but broken pieces."

Oh… I forgot; this isn't a movie; this is my life and in my life there are no happy endings and triumphant moments apparently. But, it was just an audition; not a big deal in the grand scheme of things, right?... Then why do I feel so broken? So hopeless?... I realize that this "one small thing" is actually a trigger.

My whole life has just been a series of rejections. Thirty-one years of "No!" Thirty-one years of wilderness. Thirty-one years of disgusted looks and snide comments. Thirty-one years of, "you're not what we're looking for." Thirty-one years of sticking out like a sore thumb! Thirty-one years! Thirty-one years of being taken apart piece by piece and every time closing off a little bit more of me. Thirty-one years. Pieces of me scattered across thirty-one years of rejection and enough is enough!

By the way, before those words escape your mouth… I am sick of the tired clichés that were meant to encourage. All they do is fall short at this point:

"The harder the attack, the greater the anointing,"
"Your breakthrough is closer than you know."
"Your blessing is right around the corner,"
"Praise Him in the hallway until He opens a door…"

ENOUGH!!! I'm sick of it! I literally feel like I've got nothing left to give God but broken pieces. When does my life start to look like what God promised?

Yes, I'm tired, angry and frustrated. Yes, doubt is trying to creep in. Yes, I want to throw in the towel. Yes, I want God to stop subjecting me to pain after pain after pain. I

> *"When does my life start to look like what God promised?"*

want it all to just stop!… Yet, at the end of the day, I still choose to submit to Him and His plan. Do I feel like a fool writing that? Absolutely; but, the foolishness of God is wiser than human wisdom[1]. I believe that His Word is true. Though it's hard for me to say at this time, I must hold to the truth, even when the foundation of my faith is being tested; and the truth is that God's Word will not return to Him void. It will accomplish what it was sent to do[2.] And today, God's Word is sent to encourage me; so, today, I hold onto the truth that, "Though He slay me, yet will I

---

[1] I Corinthians 1:25
[2] Isaiah 55:11

trust in Him[3]." I will remain confident in Him. Today I will trust Him even in my utter brokenness. I choose to believe that my brokenness is yielding fruit. Today, in all my frustration...I choose to pursue surrender.

Sincerely,
Tired of Being Broken...

A Proper Perspective of Rejection
(2/7/19)

Let's face it, rejection isn't easy, but it becomes easier when we finally get to the place where we live to serve and honor God and stop caring what other people think. Now, some of you may have been born with the spiritual gift of not giving a "silent but deadly wind" in a windstorm, but for the rest of us, rejection stings; so, what can we do about it? Well, I'm glad you asked. I'll tell you what I'll do about it; I'll do the only thing I'm qualified to do, point you to the cross of Christ.

Rejection was not foreign to Jesus. In the short time that He spent on earth, He became very well acquainted with it. Jesus carried a message of love, hope, healing, repentance and redemption wherever He went and people still rejected Him. He brought the cure to whatever ailed the people and the people

---

[3] Job 13:15a

4

still yelled, "Crucify Him!" So, what does He have to say to us about rejection? I'll tell you, but first…

What kind of creative would I be without including some reference to the movie The Greatest Showman? First of all, "Never Enough"???… Good Lord, what a song!!! I digress. The major theme I got from the film was that when you live for the applause of men, your life will always fall short of purpose and leave you unfulfilled. While this is not a huge revelation, it is a truth worth revisiting from time to time. But, where did we first encounter that truth about living for people?

In Galatians chapter one, the Apostle Paul was speaking to the churches in Galatia. He was expressing his disappointment that they had been so easily led astray by false teachers who were preaching a "new and improved" gospel message. In verse ten of chapter one, Paul said some very pointed and unambiguous words, "Am I now trying to win the approval of human beings, or of God? Or am I trying to please people? If I were still trying to please people, I would not be a servant of Christ."[4] Paul's words invoke a specific internal response in me: the need to examine my motives in every area of my life:

---

[4] *Galatians 1:10*

Am I writing this book because I want to impress people or to please the heart of God?

Am I leading worship because I want to regale people or because I want to touch God's heart?

Am I doing this thing, or saying that thing, because I want people to think I'm super spiritual, or because it reveals the truth of my heart toward God?

Why am I doing what I'm doing?

I know we're talking about rejection right now and you think that I've gotten off the beaten path, but actually, this is where the path starts. You see, if my motive is to impress people, then I will take rejection personally every single time; but, if my motive is God — His honor, His glory, His delight — then I understand rejection the way that Jesus did. In Luke 10:16 He said to His disciples, "Whoever listens to you listens to me; whoever rejects you rejects me; but whoever rejects me rejects him who sent me." Do you see what Jesus did there? As He was about to send His disciples out to perform miracles among the people He prepared them for the reality that everyone would not receive them well. In other words, some people would reject them. But, then Jesus told the disciples very plainly how they were to process that rejection… Don't take it personal.

Jesus addresses the innate human desire to focus on ourselves. To paraphrase, Jesus says to them "This isn't about you. You are not going in your own name; you're going in my name. But, it's not about me either because I'm going in the name of my Father!" Jesus tells His disciples outright, "Yes, people are going to reject you as you go out! But, understand that it's not you they are actually rejecting, it is God they're rejecting because you are about His business."

I know, you're probably thinking, "That's nice, Ange, but what's the implication for me?" Here it is: stop taking rejection personally. And I'm talking to me too, in fact, I'm talking to me most of all! Stop taking rejection so personally! If I'm doing what I'm doing because I want to honor God then it is God that people are rejecting and if they are rejecting God, then it's God's business to handle the rejection, not mine.

On the other hand, if I find that I'm doing what I'm doing, not because I want to honor God, but because I want to please people, then the implication of the rejection is quite different. If I am rejected by people and I find that my motive was people and not God, then I'm out of order and perhaps I needed to experience the sting of that rejection to show me that my affections and motives were misplaced. Take a moment and think about a time when you felt rejected — it could be when a relationship ended, or a family member(s) turned their back on you or even disowned you, or when you were passed over for a promotion and the list goes on and on.

Get at least one instance of rejection in your mind and then consider honestly what your goal was in that situation. In the context of a relationship, were you doing your best to win the heart and affection of that person or were you trying to honor God in your interactions and relationship with that person? Were you trying to make God happy, that person happy or yourself happy? In the context of the family turning its back, were you trying to find ways to satisfy family members, to be who they thought you should be or do what they thought you should do and you fell short or chose a different direction? Were you hell-bent on doing what you wanted, no matter the consequences and they rejected you; or were you doing something — making a choice to do or be who God created you to be and because it was not what they wanted, they rejected you? Why did you want that promotion? For your own pleasure, so you could have power, bragging rights and the corner office with the great view; or did you want that promotion because it afforded you the opportunity to bring God glory? Let's take a moment and truly examine our motives.

For me, much of the rejection I've internalized over the years was so difficult for me to overcome because I was either self-focused or people-focused.

I've spent most of my life trying to please people and win their affection or respect or esteem. But, the issue is, that's not why you and I were created.

Let's just say that somehow I performed the impossible task (I repeat, it's an impossible task; hint, hint) of pleasing every person in my life all at the same time. What exactly will I have accomplished if I didn't do what I did for God's glory? You see, we are literally created to worship God with our lives – to reflect the glory of God into the world. Thus, if I've managed to please every person in my life, but not honor God, not point folks to His glory, not worship Him at all, then haven't I just spent precious moments living meaninglessly? I might be temporarily gratified while the applause of people rings out, but when that applause stops – and it will – I am still unfulfilled and back to square one, trying to make everyone happy. You know who's never happy in that cycle? God… and me; God, because He should be receiving the glory and me, because even while that applause is ringing out, I can't enjoy it because I'm already thinking of ways to keep the applause coming.

God is calling us to examine our motives – really look at the things that we spend our time on from day to day and determine who we are trying to please. He wants us to examine who we are living our lives for, is it people, is it God or is it ourselves? If the answer is anything other than God, then we've got our motives wrong. I'm not living this life to please man. I'm not even living this life to please me! I'm living this life to please God and if He is not the catalyst behind my every action then I need to ask Him to refocus my life. Once we get our life focused in the right direction — on Him— then when rejection comes — because it is a matter of when, not if — I will be able to do what Jesus instructed His disciples to do: not take it personally, and dust my feet off and keep moving[5.]

Let's take a moment to reflect and pray. Reflect on moments where you became overwhelmed and consumed by rejection. Reflect on your motive in those moments. If you find that your motives were other people or even yourself, then repent and ask God's forgiveness for losing focus and giving others the attention that He deserves. If your motive was God, then let yourself off the hook because Jesus tells us that when we do the work of God, if people reject us, it's not really us they are rejecting, it is the God who sent us. Whatever the motive, whatever the instance of rejection, you've probably been carrying around a lie in your heart that you're not good enough and a chip on your shoulder that you have to prove to everyone that you are good enough.

To recap, as we pray today, we are repenting, we are asking God to refocus us on Him — the most

---

[5] *Matthew 10:14*

important thing—and we are asking Him to teach us not to take rejection personally.

At the back of the book in Index B you will find scriptures listed by chapter. Take a peek at the scriptures for "Surrendering Rejection" and use them for the following: I suggest meditating on one scripture a day for the next seven days and asking God to speak to you through that scripture. You may choose to use these scriptures this way, but perhaps you get to day two or three and God asks you to stick with that scripture for a bit before moving on; do whatever God tells you to do. No one is going to pop up at your front door and tell you that you're doing the activity wrong. If they do, tell 'em to come pop up at my front door and try that… I digress.

Let these scriptures guide and inform your journaling and prayer time with God each day. Ultimately, be reminded that while the world may reject us, while some people may reject us, God does not. He accepts us just as we are. In case no one in your life tells you, hear it from me as I echo God's Word, You are accepted and you are loved.

Sincerely,
In Pursuit of Surrender

P.R.I.D.: Post Rejection Identity Disorder
(11/12/19)

Back again. In my life most recently, God has been revealing some things to me. I've been experiencing some loneliness (which is normal, by the way. Sometimes, we do experience loneliness). But, then this loneliness gave way to this despairing place, and in the midst of this despairing place, I found myself crying out, quite literally, "How come nobody wants me?!" Yeah, that's a true story... But, let me give you some context.

I am what I call "single, single." That is to say that I am single because I am currently unmarried; but I'm also currently not in any semblance of a relationship. I'm not seeing anyone or getting to know anyone intentionally or otherwise. Quite frankly, I've only been on one date since my last relationship ended almost nine years ago! And, even that date was a year ago! LISTEN... my drought is having a drought!

Now that you have some context for my singleness (because we'll talk about this singleness thing a few more times before it's all said and done) let's continue. Singleness has always been a sore spot for me. I've spent most of my life feeling like the ugly duckling, the tagalong undesirable friend, or the consummate homegirl-sister-friend (think Leslie Wright from the movie Just Wright). There are many things that have contributed to the way I've thought of myself, not the least of which was low self-esteem; however, a major reason that I've felt this way for most of my life is that I've been conditioned by life to feel and to see myself this way. There are so many instances that come to mind that have helped shape me in this way. Many of those instances are from childhood because, let's face it, childhood experiences are some of the ones that stick the longest and shape us the most. We are so malleable and impressionable at those young ages and much of what we do, say and think today started in childhood whether we realize it or not.

There were some devastating rejections that I suffered growing up and although I thought myself to be a well-adjusted and healed adult, God has been showing me through recent events that there is a spirit of rejection that had attached itself to me in childhood and since then it has dug in some deep roots. As I re-read this first chapter on rejection, God began to show me that there is more work to do in order to fully heal. So, here I am, a year and a half later, back in chapter one, surrendering not just rejection, but the spirit of rejection. God is making it clear to me that unless I surrender this spirit of rejection that I've unknowingly accepted as a part of my identity, I will continue to fight this battle against rejection. As difficult as this journey will be, I'm on board with God's plan. I must get rid of the spirit of rejection because it's not who I am and quite frankly, I'm tired of believing its lies.

Recently, while talking through this battle, I confessed to my accountability partner that, without realizing it, I have been so conditioned by the spirit of rejection that I walk into every situation and every atmosphere expecting to be rejected. When I walk into an audition, like the one I discussed earlier, I expect to not be chosen. When I was in a relationship, I expected him to "come to his senses" at any moment and walk away. When I find myself interested in a man now, as a single woman, I expect that he isn't aware of my existence, or would not feel the same way. In professional situations I'd walk into pretty much every one-on-one meeting afraid that I'd be fired. These are ugly truths to unearth publicly, or privately, for that matter, but I need to put this in the light and remove the enemy's power; he has tormented me here for most of my life. The point is, I've gone into every season of my life, every opportunity, every relationship in my life expecting to be rejected sooner or later.

Do you understand how damaging that is? The spirit of rejection has literally governed my life to this point because I was unaware of its presence. Thanks be to God I'm aware now; and I refuse to sacrifice God's purpose and destiny on the altar of rejection.

I shared a few paragraphs ago about being "single, single" because it's clearly been God's doing. I know you're probably thinking,

"Dang, Ange! Conspiracy theorist, much?! You think God is conspiring against you too?!"

The answer is no, not at all; but, what I've come to understand is that God has been protecting me. You see, God knew that at this moment in my life I would need to fight this spirit—this demon—that has been torturing me all my life. He knew the time would come when I'd need to face this thing and overcome it once and for all. So, He's been protecting me from the temptation to settle for "whatever I could get," protecting me from being distracted by other non-sanctioned relationships within which I'd try to find my worth. He's been protecting me from projecting my insecurities onto some unsuspecting man because I refused to deal with them on my own. He's been protecting me . . . from me.

Early on in my singleness I used to think that I was cursed because no man really even showed much interest; however, I came to understand that God had a plan and was actually guarding me; keeping me hidden, if you will, because there were some things He wanted to heal in me before releasing me to relationship and marriage. In fact, until this very moment, I didn't even realize that the reason I've been so vexed by being single is because I've viewed my "single, single" status as a wholesale rejection.

Now, years later, I finally understand God's strategy and I see what He's been preparing me for. He's been getting me ready for this final battle. You see, He allowed me to walk through years of feeling alone and unwanted so that I could finally become aware that single does not mean undesirable. He needed me to comprehend and accept that unless I understand that He's made me enough on my own, I'll never understand my full worth and value in relationship and marriage. He needed me to understand that my value has nothing to do with marital status, or whomever accepts, or rejects me. He needed me to understand that my worth and identity are always and only rooted in Him—not in people, positions, relationship, or people's opinions—only in Him. In order to set me up to overcome, though, God needed to allow me to experience the fullness of the weight of the spirit of rejection and the ways in which it has shaped me. He needed me to look back at a parted Red Sea and see the Egyptians of my past bearing down on me so that He could say, "You will never see these enemies again[6]."

God allowed me to be "single, single" for so long because He needed me to see that all that I needed and have been seeking (love, attention, affection, to be

---

[6] *Exodus 14:13*

known, acceptance, etc.) is found in Him. God desires to make me whole in singleness; otherwise, I might get caught up believing that a man completed me; and ain't nobody got time for that!

Destiny and purpose are waiting on me to walk in wholeness. Lives are attached to me walking in wholeness. The enemy desired to take me to this despairing place to break me — to destroy me. But, God allowed me into this despairing place so that I would see that it can't break me because He made me to conquer it. What the enemy meant for evil, God meant for what is now being accomplished — the saving of many lives[7].

Some are wondering why I would be so transparent and right at the beginning of this book and the answer is because my life is not my own. Everything that has happened, is happening and will happen in my life is for the sharing, that through my testimony God might deliver others. I don't have time to be embarrassed about my testimony, nor any of the struggles I currently walk through. God's got a purpose in mind for me and if I'm going to walk in it, then pride has to die. Therefore, I'll be as real and transparent as I need to be in order that

> *"Not only does rejection no longer define me, it no longer even describes me."*

[7] *Genesis 50:20*

someone else might see my life and examine their own to see how God is actually delivering them in the midst of what they thought would destroy them.

I've been subject to the spirit of rejection long enough. No more. God calls me whole; that's who I am. The enemy no longer gets to define me. I am accepted by God. I am fully known by God and loved as I am. I had become so accustomed to rejection that I started to believe that rejection was a part of my name, but now I know the truth. Not only does rejection no longer define me, it no longer even describes me. You see, this battle against rejection really does come back to having a proper perspective. A proper perspective of rejection… but also, a proper perspective of self. If I know, beyond the shadow of a doubt, who I am, I can't be convinced of a lie. I am whole; I am complete, lacking nothing. I am loved. I am accepted. So are you.

Sincerely,
In Pursuit of Surrender

"… Yet will I trust Him."
~Job

Surrendering In The Midst Of Pain
(2/12/2017)

Today was better than yesterday. When you're a worship leader, you are expected to "always be on." My prayer before worship was to not just go through the motions. I prayed that I would truly worship God in light of my pain, and not in spite of it. I wanted to truly worship through brokenness and not mask it as usual.

> *"I want my worship to be true no matter the circumstance."*

I'm tired of going through the motions whenever I'm struggling, or hurting, or at odds with God. But, I guess the only way for that to be tested is to go through trying circumstances. It is possible to worship in the midst of pain, devastation, fear, and disappointment; but, I wouldn't have known it if He didn't allow me to be tested to my breaking point.

Now I know why everyone looked at Job like he was crazy. In the midst of his most excruciating test he declared, "Though He slay me yet will I trust Him." And if Job could press through that, then surely I can press through this. Though you slay me, yet will I trust you, God.

Sincerely,

Broken…But In Pursuit of Surrender

"Everything changes when I say, 'Thank you'."
~Anthony Evans, Everything Changes

Surrendering My Mind
(2/22/2017)

How do I choose worship when everything isn't all peaches n' cream? Well, first, I recognize that I have a choice, but, for sure, it's easier said than done. If I'm honest, it is difficult to look all around at my life and see all of the promises that haven't yet manifested and still choose worship. I know the old hymn says to "count your many blessings," but it's so much easier to notice and count the many things that I don't yet have.

I guess what I'm saying is that what's necessary is a surrendering of our minds. It is so easy to focus on the negative; but, that should be our first clue, it's very seldom that what God is asking is easy. That's because what God requires comes through the Holy Spirit which communicates to our spirit. Galatians 5:17 says, "The sinful nature wants to do evil, which is just the opposite of what the Spirit wants. And the Spirit gives us desires that are the opposite of what the sinful nature desires. These two forces [The Spirit and the flesh] are constantly fighting each other, so you are not free to carry out your good intentions." (NLT) There you have it. We are constantly warring internally. Every day there is a civil war and most days we've allowed the flesh to win. We've chosen to focus on the negative. Anthony Evans, Jr. has a song on his album "Back to Life" that says, "Everything changes when I say thank you." We've always got at least one reason to be thankful.

> "... it is difficult to look all around at my life and see all of the promises that haven't yet manifested
>
> and still choose worship."

You may be thinking, "So, how do I choose differently than I've chosen for the last twenty or forty or eighty years? How do I suddenly start to choose to focus on the good instead of the bad — what I do have, instead of what I don't have?" Listen, God is not Dumbledore and we are not young Harry Potters, Hermiones and Rons.[8] There is no magic

---

[8] In reference to the Harry Potter book/movie series written by J.K. Rowling. Harry and Ron are young wizards in training and Hermione is a young witch in training. Dumbledore is a revered master wizard. This

involved here. The simple answer is that we take it one battle at a time. From now on, we decide that when we want to focus on what God hasn't done or given us, we'll stop ourselves smack dab in the middle of that thought, take it captive and then hold it up under The Light—the Word of God[9].

Ask yourself: Does this thought come from God? Does this look and sound like something God wants me to meditate on?

If your answer to those questions is, "no," then chuck those sneaky jokers (negative thoughts) and exchange them for some moments of thanks. Begin to recall the good that God has done for you that you didn't deserve and the bad that He's held back time and time again. Choose to focus on better.

I earnestly believe that when we begin to do that consistently, everything will change. I'm not telling you to do something that I've mastered years ago. I'm not telling you to power through some struggle from which I'm so far removed. I am sharing with you, in real-time, the struggle that God is walking me through. I'm inviting you to be a walking partner so you don't have to walk it out alone. I believe God has given us everything we need to take captive every thought and make them obedient to Jesus Christ.

---

reference is simply used to make it clear that there's no magic solution in this process.
[9] *2 Corinthians 10:5*

As we break for prayer, I challenge you to ask God to: Help you identify negative thoughts and take them captive as soon as they arise…[10]

Sincerely,
In Pursuit of Surrender

45 Reasons

Philippians 4:8-9 says, "Finally, brothers and sisters, whatever is true, whatever is noble, whatever is right, whatever is pure, whatever is lovely, whatever is admirable—if anything is excellent or praiseworthy—think about such things. Whatever you have learned or received or heard from me, or seen in me—put it into practice. And the God of peace will be with you."

I want to challenge you to do something different this week, starting today. If we are going to be serious about surrendering to God, we can't just talk about it and then move on; no, we have to do something different[11]. So, today, turn to a fresh page in your journal[12], turn on some worship music and give yourself a minute to listen to the words and allow them to carry you into the presence of God. While in

---

[10] For full list of prayer points, turn to page 11 in your IPoS Journal.

[11] *James 1:22-25*

[12] Or page 15 in your IPoS Journal

His presence, think about ten reasons you have to be thankful today; write down all ten in your journal. Then for the next five days, come back and add five reasons each day. Make sure that you don't repeat anything; you want a fresh five reasons every day. These can be "old" reasons — things He's done for you in years past — or new reasons — things He's recently done. Then, on day seven, write out another ten reasons. At the end of seven days, you will have written 45 reasons to be grateful to God.

Finally, God wants us to be fully invested in this surrender process, so, head to your local dollar store or Target, (pronounced Tar-zjay) if you're feeling extra glamorous and sacrificial, and buy an 8x10 picture frame, at least. You can go bigger if you'd like. You are going to use this frame to prominently display your 45 Reasons somewhere in your home. You can do this however artistically or practically you'd like. For example you could list your 45 Reasons typed and double spaced on a sheet of paper OR if you are so inclined, you could create an artistic rendering of your list, maybe find an adult coloring page and write your reasons there. The possibilities are endless, but the point is simple: you want to give yourself a visual reminder of these 45 Reasons that you have to be grateful to God; and every time you see your reasons you're gonna be reminded that, these are just one week's worth of thanks — really, just one fraction of what you've got to be thankful for in the space of one week. This visual will help you remember that no matter what may be going on in your life, no matter how bad, you still have AT LEAST 45 Reasons to be thankful to God.

The object of this exercise is to get your mind working in the opposite direction. Naturally, our minds gravitate to and focus on negative things. This exercise will help jump start a reversal of our thought process, but it only works if you continue it beyond this one week. Before you get started, let's pray by asking God to help us refocus our minds. Let's ask Him to bring back to our remembrance the things that He's done, the battles He's won, the ways He's provided, and so on. Let's ask Him to help us shift our focus from us to Him and how He is present in each and every day. Let's gear up and pray, then let's go to work!

Sincerely,
In Pursuit of Surrender

"Love is patient..."
~1 Cor. 13:4

Surrendering To Perfect Love
(2/28/17)

Today is one of those "gentle reminder" days. Sometimes God has to show me tough love because I can be so hard-headed. Then, some days, He knows that all I need is a gentle reminder. My "Verse of the Day" today was 1 Cor. 13:4-5 and it's the first three words that gripped me. Today, God has reminded me that love is patient. The verse doesn't say that love is patient for a while and then gets tired of waiting and so it gives up. In fact, verse seven says that love never gives up. Love is patient and love never gives up!

For a while now I've felt like I was justified in my feelings. I've been waiting for years for God's promises to come to pass. Promises regarding my career, relationships, ministry calling, education; so many promises for which I've been waiting. And waiting and waiting and waiting. Oh, and did I mention, waiting?! So, yeah, I felt like I was absolutely justified when I got tired and dissolved into tears and asked God , "How long?!" But, the scripture says that love is patient and love never gives up! If I love God — and I do, in case you were wondering — then love overrides impatience.

Love overrides fear. Love overrides frustration. Love is patient and never fails! Love does not expire! Love is not conditional! Therefore, I've got to choose, do I want to love God more or do I want what I want more? Do I want to love God more or do I want to see advancement in my career more? Do I want to love God more or do I want to be married on my own timeline more? Do I love God more or do I want to be comfortable more?

When I see the choices clearly laid out this way, the decision is easy. I choose God. I choose to love God more. I make this choice recognizing that it will not always be easy. I make this choice recognizing that the wait will be frustrating at times but when it gets frustrating I will remind myself that Love is patient. Love is kind. Love is not jealous, boastful, proud or rude. It does not demand its own way... Stop and reflect on that for a moment, Love does not demand its own way...... I'll repeat it to myself once more (maybe, you don't need the repetition, but I certainly do)... Love does NOT demand its own way!... Yyyyyyup; that stings a bit. Love is not irritable and it keeps no record of wrongs. It does not rejoice about injustice but rejoices whenever the truth wins out. Love never gives up, never loses faith, is always hopeful and endures through every circumstance... Love will last forever[13].

I think if I keep reminding myself of these truths I'll be able to wait just a while longer because, inherent in Love, is trust. So, if I love God — and I do, remember — then I must be willing to trust God.

Today, I will meditate on the truth that Love is patient. I trust God not because the Bible says I should, but, because I love Him. And so . . . I wait, patiently.

Sincerely,
In Pursuit of Surrender

Watchmen

I love Psalm 130:5-6 for multiple reasons. First, on a surface level, when I read these verses in the NIV, which is my go-to translation at the time of this writing, it just sounds so doggone poetic; and as a wordsmith myself, I'm a sucker for poetry. But, secondly, this has become one of my favorite passages of scripture because it paints the picture of my life.

My life, especially the last seven years of it, has been a series of seasons that have had one thing in common... Waiting. Psalm 130:5-6 reads, "I wait for the Lord, my whole being waits, and in His word I

---

[13] *1 Corinthians 13:4-7 adapted slightly from the NLT*

put my hope. I wait for the Lord more than watchmen wait for the morning, more than watchmen wait for the morning." God has been doing a lot of speaking and confirming in these last several years. He's spoken through His Holy Word, He's spoken by way of prophetic utterances flowing through people who don't know me from Adam and Eve in The Garden, He's

> *. . . I'm going to have to lose myself in the wait."*

spoken through preached words, His Word has borne witness in my spirit as I've sought Him in my private time.

He's been a speaking, brotha!...
    Father?....
        Lord? — yeah, let's go with that one.

He's been a speaking Lord! I have spent the last several years listening for His voice and taking notes. I've received the words that He's spoken to me. I've prayed over them. I've prayed about what part He wants me to play in bringing His Word to pass, if any. Yet, the truth remains, that I am still awaiting the manifestation of the vast majority of His Words spoken over me.

As you can imagine, it has been incredibly frustrating. God has spoken some really awesome and amazing things over my life; and I am so excited to walk in the fullness of what He's spoken, but I'm in a relentless holding pattern. I've wanted to give up at times, I've wanted to make things happen on my own. I've cried, I've prayed, I've complained, I've gotten over it, and then gone through the cycle all over again more times than I care to count or admit. The point is, I'm still waiting. This waiting doesn't always feel good, but I made a decision that I am going to walk in and receive everything that God has spoken over me. The catch is, if I'm going to walk in the fullness of my calling and blessing, I'm going to have to lose myself in the wait.

You see, while I'm waiting to see God's promises manifest in my life, He's waiting for me to let go of who I had become in favor of who He created me to be from the beginning. God intends that every bit of calling, promise and blessing that was spoken over me will come to pass, but before I can walk in the fullness of it, I have to shed the layers of masks that the enemy has put on me over the years. I can't walk into purpose with a disguise on. It's sort of like a door that is only opened via facial recognition; I can't open those doors with my name on them if I'm still wearing the masks that I hid behind two or five or ten years ago. Access denied.[14] So, as I wait, I have been submitting to God, so that He could remove the

_____

14 More about this later

masks and get to His original design of me. In the process, He had to introduce me to me. As God peels back the layers, I'm getting to see God's original design. I'm loving what I see, who I see. Am I perfect? Sure. I'm imperfectly perfect, exactly who God wants me to be in this season of my life, flaws and all, so that He can get the glory through me.

Why did I go on that tangent? Because what I'm getting at is that this waiting has a purpose. I know you're tired. Me too. I know you're frustrated. Me too. I know you want to get to the other side of this breakthrough. Me too. I know you are wondering will the pain, the lack, the hallway, the season ever end. I'm here to tell you that it will; and it will give way to new season, new anointing, new confidence, which will give way to new pains, new hallways and new seasons.

I encourage you to surrender to God in the wait because there will be more waiting in your life; and if you learn to surrender now, you won't have to learn later. So, how do we surrender in the wait? We start by taking the focus off of ourselves. In just a moment I'm going to invite you to pray and as you pray, there are a few things I suggest you ask God:

- God, what do YOU want to do in this season?

- God, what do you want me to learn/get in this season?...[15]

Take a few moments to grab your prayer journal, get your worship music going and let's pray. But don't forget that a vital part of prayer is listening after we've made our petitions known. So, after you spend moments speaking or writing in prayer, don't get up without spending time being still, being quiet, silencing your mind and just listening.

Again, Psalm 130:5-6 says, "I wait for the Lord, my whole being waits, and in His word I put my hope. I wait for the Lord more than watchmen wait for the morning, more than watchmen wait for the morning." Habakkuk 2:1 says, "I will stand at my watch and station myself on the ramparts; I will look to see what He will say to me, and what answer I am to give to this complaint."

Let's not ask God these crucial questions and then disrespect Him by walking away. Let's stop and position ourselves to listen and hear from Him.

Sincerely,
In Pursuit of Surrender

---

[15] For full list of prayer foci, turn to page 20 in your IPoS Journal.

"Walking around fearful. What if someone finds out the truth; that I'm shattered, pieced together by the love of You. Not worthy of Your attention; I'm so guilty and ashamed.
Please don't use me.
No, You can't use me."
~Casey J, Journal

Surrendering My Excuses
(3/6/17)

Since the moment God began to reveal His purpose in my life until this present moment, I've probably spent at least half of my time telling myself and trying to convince God of why I couldn't, can't or shouldn't do it. The more I gave excuses, the more He revealed; and the more He revealed, the bigger my calling became; and the bigger my calling became, the more excuses I had about why I wasn't the right one to carry it. Now first of all, I know that was like the longest run-on sentence known to man but it was necessary to demonstrate what my life looked like — a huge run-on sentence — and the only place it was running was in circles. In retrospect, I'm filled with gratitude for God's patience; I mean, talk about Love is patient. I can hear myself giving God excuse after excuse and to Him I must've sounded like Moses.

By the time we reach chapter four of Exodus, Moses has already played a round of "I'm not worthy" and a round of "What if?" Nevertheless, God had an answer for it all. So, when chapter four picks up, Moses is on round two and he tries everything. Grasping at straws, he asks, "What if they don't believe me?" But, God has all of the bases covered, and that's no surprise. When he can't find a hole in God's plan and purpose for him, Moses just tries disqualifying himself from the purpose altogether. I've been there!

- "I'm not good enough."
- "So and so is better than I am."
- "No one cares what I have to say."

The list goes on and on. So, Moses tried it, but God wasn't having it. Not any of it. Moses says,

"I don't speak well, God, so you should probably send someone more eloquent." But God was ready. God essentially says to Moses, "Seriously?! This is what you're gonna go with? You think I don't know how you speak? I created you. I'm the one who decides who is deaf and who hears. I am the one who gave you a mouth to speak."

There is a reason for everything that God allows. I truly believe that even if Moses wasn't an eloquent speaker (which is debatable[16]), the entire reason God created Moses, then, to speak ineloquently was because He wanted to make sure that when Moses went back to speak to Pharaoh and all the other people that knew him growing up, and they heard him speak with power and authority, they would know that it was nothing but the all-powerful God who could have sent him.

"God doesn't operate in possibilities.

He doesn't need to."

The point I'm making is that our excuses are not a surprise to God. They don't catch Him off guard and, make no mistake, every excuse that we could possibly come up with in our finite minds was already seen and prepared for by our infinite God. So, it's best to abandon our excuses about why we can't

---

[16] *Acts 7:22* says that Moses was mighty in both speech and action. It is quite possible, then, that Moses just had a skewed perception of himself when we see him in Exodus. It is also possible that when Stephen speaks of Moses in Acts 7:22, he may mean that ultimately Moses became known as being mighty in speech based on his function as the prophet (mouthpiece) for God. We don't really know...

or shouldn't be the one that God uses for His purposes. And the fact of the matter is, whatever your excuse, you're probably right! You aren't worthy. You may not be eloquent enough. You probably are more comfortable in the background... Me too, to all of the above. But, the truth is that's all a part of the reason God chose us. Did you catch that? God doesn't just prepare beforehand for the "possibility" of a deficiency or excuse arising. God doesn't operate in possibilities. He doesn't need to. God has so well-crafted His plans for us that His plans include those deficiencies that lead to excuses! In other words, God knows our excuses, even before we've formulated them and He has worked the deficiencies that spawn those excuses into His plan so that He gets the glory!

Today I'm focusing on surrendering my excuses. I'm pulling out my white flag filled with excuses and I'm waving it because God created His plan and purpose for my life in light of all my deficiencies and excuses, not in spite of them. Yeah... He's just that good. Selah. Let's meditate and reflect on that today. We can trust the God who has a track record of being that thorough, especially when that same record proves that He never fails.

Sincerely,
In Pursuit of Surrender

The Reboot
January 2019

Today, God led me to Jeremiah chapter one, as He spoke to me so clearly in those verses, He reminded me of this same "Chapter Five: Surrendering Excuses" Word that He gave me last March. In Jeremiah 1:6 the writer says to God, "I do not know how to speak; I am too young." Now, in verses four and five, God minces no words. He tells Jeremiah, plain and simple, that He has called him to be a prophet to speak to the nations. God tells Jeremiah that He's put a lot of thought and planning into Jeremiah's purpose. To paraphrase, God essentially says, "Before I formed you in the womb I knew you, before you were born I set you apart; I appointed you as a prophet to the nations."

"What is in us responds to

who created us."

God is saying to Jeremiah, "before you were even a glimmer in your parents' eyes, you were a glimmer in mine. I mapped you out in my mind before I knit you together inside your mother's womb. I thought through every detail of your life, of your being. I thought about what I wanted you to do in the earth, about the need that I wanted you to meet and in light of that purpose, I equipped you perfectly to do just that."

In response to that, Jeremiah offered God his excuses. What I love about God is the way in which he responds to Jeremiah. It is the same way in which He responded to Moses so many years before. In response to their insecurities and perceived deficiencies God reassures them of His own "who-ness." God reminds Moses that He is the one that created him and then He tells Moses that He will go with him and tell him what to say. God reassures Jeremiah that he can put his excuses away because He, Himself, would be with Jeremiah and tell him where to go and what to say.

I love that God's answer to my insecurities, imperfections and perceived deficiencies is Himself. When I get so focused on me—what I can't do, what I shouldn't do and what I'm not worthy or equipped or good enough to do, God responds by shifting my focus to who He is. Why? Because, who He is, is enough. Who He is, is more than enough to compensate for my imperfections. Who He is, is able to cover ALL of who I am. So, God just gently refocuses me. You see, God didn't call us so that we could deliberate and decide if that's what we are best suited to do. He didn't call us so that we could audition His purpose in our lives and then reject or accept it based on our preferences.

Before we became aware of God's calling in our lives, He created us to complete it, to fulfill it. He created us—crafted us—in such a way that everything that we needed to accomplish His purpose was in us; IS in us. He crafted us so well that what we'd need in different seasons in order to walk in purpose would time-release in us, like a medicine. He placed time-released anointing in us so that He could use us as a medicine in a broken, bruised, sick, hurting and dying world. But, you see the active ingredient for the time-released anointing in any given season of our lives is His presence. What is in us responds to who created us. He is the necessary element. There can be no proper chemical reaction without the proper catalyst and He is it. For us to be able to walk in calling and purpose, we must do it in Him. The result, when we try to shoulder the weight of carrying out His purpose in our lives is that we turn internally. We focus on our perceived abilities and inabilities, our inadequacies. We focus on us. Consequently, God reminds us over and over again in His Word—Moses and Jeremiah are just two such instances — that as long as we are focused on what we cannot do, we will never have the opportunity to see what He can do.

Today, be encouraged. Don't let excuses keep you from seeing all that God desires to do through you. No matter what your excuse, God took time to speak a Word to that excuse before you were ever formed in the womb. He took time to craft you so well that when your "can't" met up with His "can", they would catalyze and produce His Will. But, you've got to be willing to facilitate the meeting. Are you willing to surrender your excuses to Him today?

Sincerely,
In Pursuit of Surrender

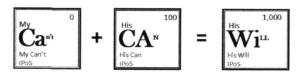

#SimpleEquation

Abandon Excuses, All Who Enter Here
(2/11/19)

In Dante's Inferno[17], Dante Alighieri writes about his journey through hell. In the epic poem he writes about the inscription he sees above the gates of hell, "Lasciate ogne speranza, voi ch'intrate," which, in English, means, "Abandon hope, all ye who enter here." That is to say that all who find themselves entering into the gates of hell should check their hope at the door because once through those gates, they'll have no use for it.

Similarly, as God is calling us higher in this surrender journey, He's calling us to walk fully in purpose. He is saying to us, "Abandon excuses, all you who enter here." God is saying to us that when we commit to walking according to His plan, we have no use for excuses, except, of course, to use them as stepping stools to boost us up to the next level. You see, excuses sometimes keep us bound and stagnant for years, for decades. We were not meant to stagnate, to atrophy and die here. We were meant to walk victoriously, boldly, in authority to win souls for The Kingdom. When we get stuck on our 'buts' we begin to backpedal slowly until we come to a complete halt. You and I were meant for more than where we are.

---

[17] *Inferno* is the first part of the epic poem *Divine Comedy* completed by Dante Alighieri in 1320 A.D.

This week, we're gonna take time to look at some folks who had excuses too, but our goal will be to see past their excuses to get to their uses. We are going to look at all the reasons why they "should not" have been used and then hold that in tension with what God actually did through them. The goal is to get into your mind the truth that there is nothing that can thwart the plan of God[18], not even our 'buts.' After examining the excuses of those that God chose to use in the Bible for six days, we're going to write down our own excuses on day seven.

What's been holding you back from walking in the fullness of your identity, purpose and calling? Is it people's opinions? Your past? Your temperament and personality style? Your feelings of inadequacy? Your limitations? Fear? What is it; be honest. What's keeping you from fully accepting God's calling? On day seven, that's what we're going to examine. That's what we're going to admit; and that's what we're going to surrender.

For every day leading up to our day of surrender, we're going to pray that God would give us courage to face those excuses, to admit and surrender them to Him. Then we're going to pray that He teaches us to leave them at His feet and not pick them back up again. God has called us to walk in freedom; that freedom comes in our surrender. I'll probably repeat

---

[18] *Job 42:2*

this throughout this book; but that's because God wants to imprint that truth in your heart.

Your freedom comes through surrender. The enemy of our souls knows this and he would love nothing more than for us to continue to be bound; however, "whom the Son sets free is free indeed.[19]" So, here's the truth, my friend: you, ma'am; you, sir, are already free; you need only take possession of your freedom. Christ already made you free. He's already made freedom available, but you and I have to choose to possess it and live it out. Me? I choose freedom, which means my excuses have to die. What about you?

Sincerely,
In Pursuit of Surrender

***

Head over to page 25 in your IPoS Journal and choose one track to follow for the next six days.
On day seven, turn to Surrender In Action on page 26 of your journal to complete the activity for this chapter.

Track One: Moses
Track Two: Paul & Peter

---

[19] *John 8:36*

"Why am I still fighting?"
"Haven't I earned some grace, favor and rest?!"

Surrendering In The Fight
(3/8/17)

"I'm just tired! I'm so tired!" I sobbed
uncontrollably. "I'm so tired of fighting. When do I
get to come off of the battlefield and just rest?! I'm so
tired!"

I had just left the platform after leading worship
for the third time that Sunday and for the first time I
was very aware that I was just going through the
motions and that I had been for some weeks, at least. I
was frustrated for several reasons and when I became
aware of the inauthenticity of my worship, it was
painful. I hated the feeling of going through the
motions. My heart wasn't in the worship, but worship
must go on, right? People still needed to be led in
worship; the atmosphere still had to be set and I still
had to be in place and "on" to facilitate that, right? I
hated that my true worship had been reduced to a
sequence of well-placed smiles, hand raises, clichés
and annoyingly familiar exhortations. It wasn't my
intention to just go through the motions, yet here I
was faking it until I could make it. But the problem
that I pondered... no, that I agonized over on the

seemingly long walk from the platform to my office downstairs was that I was pretty sure I wouldn't make it.

I finally made it to my office. As I sat at my desk I was overwhelmed by the utter despair of hopelessness — that helpless, sinking feeling in the pit of your stomach that comes when you've been as faithful as you possibly can — completely committed to the plan and submitted to the process — on the battlefield fighting with everything you've got but then you realize that there's no extraction plan. There's no contingency to pull you out of the battle if the fight gets too intense.

There I was, smack dab in the heat of battle. I had run out of viable ammo. I was firing blanks, exhausted from the fight, entrenched and surrounded in the battle zone. I radioed for extraction and as I anxiously awaited a response, all I heard was static. Then a voice crackled in and out across the frequency, "No extraction plan. Repeat. No extraction."

Then more static.
Nothingness.
Radio silence.
What did I sign up for?

The floodgates broke open and thankfully, one of my sister-friends was there to let me get it out and encourage me. I was exhausted from the fight and wanted desperately for this season of my life to be over. Yet, God was adamant that there would be no extraction, no "ruby slippers, no place like home" option. This was the time where I had to learn how to worship in the valley instead of just going through the motions. There was something I needed to learn and because He loved me, He wouldn't let me out until I got it.

In retrospect, there were several lessons gleaned from this moment. But, as I reflect on it now the lesson that God is pointing out to me is that I need to surrender in the fight.

"Wait. Timeout. Say what, God?!"

Yup, you read that right. He's asking me to surrender in the fight—no, not to the enemy, but to Him. As I reflect on that day, I see clearly how I thought I was fully submitted to the process, but, it turns out, I was only submitted until discomfort and pain set in. I was on the battlefield fighting the enemy and when I became uncomfortable with my marching orders and how long the battle was raging on, I turned and began to fight my own teammate! That's right; friendly fire! I turned on Him in the middle of the battle and questioned: "Why would you leave me in here this long?! Haven't I been faithful enough? When are you going to end this? Why am I still fighting? Haven't I earned grace, favor and rest?!"

> *"... my faithfulness is what*
>
> *God deserves,*
>
> *not the down payment on some divine layaway plan ..."*

Holy Shrimp; did you see that entitlement come rearing its ugly head?! Clearly that was the pain and frustration speaking, but it's still alarming because if I was thinking it, then it was in me. I know that I could never earn or deserve anything but wrath and judgment from God, yet when the going got tough, I see that there was something in me that felt as though God owed me something in exchange for my faithfulness. If I'm completely honest, I still find myself having to catch those thoughts trying to slip into and permeate my mind occasionally. In truth, I know that it's quite the opposite. God doesn't owe me anything. It's me who owes Him everything; thus, my faithfulness is what God deserves, not the down payment on some divine layaway plan; and though I don't and never could deserve it, God still chooses to work all things for my good and His glory.

Today I'm choosing to surrender in the fight. I choose to stop fighting God and to focus all of my efforts on fighting the true enemy. I choose to stop swimming against the stream and go with God's flow; and I believe that when I do that, I'll see that there's more in me than I thought. There's more hope in me. There's more faith in me, and there is more fight in me when I fight alongside my help instead of against Him.

Sincerely,
In Pursuit of Surrender

Friendly Fire

In what areas of your life have you been fighting God? Is it your calling? Has He been showing you what He wants to do through you, and it's scaring you? Has He been asking you to let go of a toxic relationship or even a good relationship that is just a distraction—a relationship to which He has not called you? Are you like me, fighting against God's timing? Where have you been fighting God in your life? Be honest. Has He asked you to go somewhere, remain somewhere, do something, or say something that makes you uncomfortable?

What if I told you that the reason you are so exhausted, the reason why you're so spiritually, emotionally and physically tired is that you've been trying to fight the enemy AND God at the same time? What if I told you that the reason you seem to keep losing this spiritual battle is that your energy is divided? You could be thriving so much more and crying so much less if you'd just throw up your hands. There is a better way to battle; and it is surrender. The key to being able to surrender in the fight is to remember that my teammate knows what's best for me; He is always moving me toward that desired end. Do you know the heart of your teammate, Our Father?

We are going to see what the Bible tells us about the Father's heart toward us and then we're going to create another visual to help us remember to stop fighting our teammate. For every area of your life where you've been fighting God, we're going to make a white flag. Now, if you're crafty, you can make the flags; if you're less crafty, you can purchase some white flags. They can be as cute or as rugged as you'd like. The point is, you need some white flags, one for every area of your life where you've been fighting against God. Next, you're going to take a marker and write that thing on the flag. For example, I might write, "*kairos/chronos*," on my flag as a reminder that I fight most often against God's timing in my life. God operates on *kairos*, but I get stuck on *chronos*. Make sense? (Don't worry, we'll unpack this *kairos/chronos* struggle more later). Now, using a red marker, draw a circle around your struggle, and then draw a line going through it. At the bottom of your flag, you're going to write down one or more of the scripture addresses listed for this chapter in Index B at the back of your book. Maybe there is another scripture that comes to mind to remind you of the Father's love and plan for you; you can use that scripture too.

But, don't just write down these scriptures; hide them in your heart so that when the enemy comes calling you've got God's Word hidden in your heart to speak in response to the enemy! In this rapidly growing "cancel culture" we live in, we are going to use these visual reminders to cancel out what we always should have —  those meaningless battles that have kept us exhausted and entrenched. Let's surrender to God in the fight!

Sincerely,
In Pursuit of Surrender

"Twenty-five years?!
I had to wait twenty-five whole years?!"
~ Probably Abraham, DEFINITELY Sarah

Surrendering In The Wait
(3/13/17)

Abraham had to have been the king of waiting.
God made and reaffirmed His covenant with
Abraham three times before Isaac was born, a period
of about twenty-five years... twenty-five years! The
Bible says that God came to Abraham and told him to
pick up everything and move to another place. He
didn't even give specifics. God said to pick up
everything and go to this new region and I will bless
you and make you famous; and I will make you a
blessing to others. And Abraham did it! No questions
or hesitations from Abraham are recorded in the
Bible; he just went — obedience. Years later God
reaffirms his covenant with Abraham and expounds
upon it. This time God promises that Abraham's
offspring would be too numerous to count; however,
Abraham's wife Sarah was barren. That didn't matter
to Abraham. Genesis 15:6 says that when God told
Abraham, "Abraham believed the Lord." Some years
later Abraham and Sarah still had no child and
decided to help God's plan along by inserting Hagar,
Sarah's servant, into the mix. A child was produced,

but God came back and said that this child was not the promise-bearer. God assured Abraham that Sarah, would bear a child and that child would bear the promise; this time He gave Abraham a time frame for the coming of his covenant heir and a premise to the promise: circumcision. Abraham immediately obeyed.

As I revisit the account of Abraham's faith, I am encouraged but also challenged. Twenty-five years, Abraham waited for the fulfillment of just a part of the promise. Abraham also had to be okay with the fact that he would never physically see the rest of the promise. I'll be honest, my flesh is bothered by the question, "What if God made me wait twenty-five years to see the promises He has spoken to me?" Truth be told, it's only been a few years and doubt has already slipped in more than once. Prayerfully, it won't take twenty-five years for me to see the manifestation of God's promises in my life; but just in case it does, today I'm praying for the grace to wait faithfully.

I've spent the last several years waiting impatiently or with an arrogant sense of entitlement that left me frustrated and angry when I didn't see the promises when or how I desired. Nonetheless, I've learned something at every step of the journey. Today, I just want to be able to enjoy the season I'm in with patient expectation for what He's promised. I've done the bratty, impatient thing and I'm over it. My prayer today is that He would help me to continue waiting, but this time, with grace. I don't know what promises you're waiting to see made manifest in your life, but, I'm also praying that God would give you the grace to wait... Patiently.

Sincerely,
In Pursuit of Surrender

Grace to Wait
By Angelique A. Strothers

I've waited most impatiently
For what You said You'd do
But I've forgotten, You don't owe
It's me who does owe You

So teach me to wait patiently
With praise and smiling face
I humbly ask, My Loving Father
Give Me Grace to Wait

"...it's not comfortable for a reptile to separate itself from what has become a part of it. It's the same with us."

Surrendering To Shedding
(3/22/17)

It seems an odd thing to say that we need to surrender to shedding, but, it is quite true. In the New Living Translation (NLT) of the Bible, 2 Corinthians 5:17 reads, "This means that anyone who belongs to Christ has become a new person. The old life is gone; a new life has begun." When I think of that scripture, the image that comes to mind is that of a reptile shedding its skin. What's particularly appropriate about that analogy is that when reptiles shed, the process is ongoing. When you examine the Greek word for creature, kitsis, you'll see that it means something that's been created. But, kitsis also carries the connotation of creating; that is, the ongoing process of creation. I've always viewed that scripture as a "one and done" kind of deal. It made sense that when I gave my life to Christ, He made me new, but when I think about all of the growing pains I've gone through and continue to go through since then, it makes even more sense that He is constantly making me a new creature; because, let's face it, I'm a hot mess and I require extensive re-creation.

With the truth of this ongoing process in mind, I also have to admit that growth is uncomfortable sometimes. Experts will tell you that when a reptile sheds, it can become very irritable and reclusive. The cause, I'm willing to bet, is that it is not comfortable for a reptile to separate itself from what has become a part of it. It's the same with us. When God is inviting us to grow, it requires that we let go of what has become a part of us. The question is, why would He require something so painful? The answer is that what has become a part of us can no longer support and sustain us in the next season.

Can you imagine being a reptile in those days and weeks before shedding time? You're getting bigger, but because of the old skin that sustained and protected you in the last season, you can't stretch out to your full potential. You're uncomfortable because the skin you're in is too tight. It's too restrictive. It's now hindering you more than it's helping. Perhaps you limit your movements because doing all of the things you used to do is too painful for you. You even stop eating regularly because digestion becomes yet another uncomfortable process. You are faced with a difficult choice: live in constant pain, restriction and discomfort OR push through some temporary pain and discomfort in order to grow to your full potential.

It's the same for us spiritually. We experience life in seasons. In any given season we should be growing; sometimes the growth comes through testing and sometimes pain. Still, other times, it's quiet, God-guided reflection and introspection. Still, sometimes the growth comes when God allows us to learn from our mistakes. The point is that in every season we are learning and growing. Once we've gotten everything that God intended for us in that season, once we've grown out of all that season has provided, we start to feel the restlessness in our spirit.

We might get uncomfortable and feel like we're being suffocated or get irritable depending on what season we're leaving, what season we're entering and how the transition period looks. Perhaps we limit the amount of spiritual food we take in because every time we "eat" it hurts or causes more discomfort. Maybe we withdraw from fellowship with our brothers and sisters because it requires energy and effort and all we really want to do is use all our energy and effort to break out of this uncomfortable, painful, irritating place. Frankly, the last thing we need and want is for yet another person to placate us yet again with those well-meant, but tired clichés:

> *"This too shall pass."*
> *"Weeping endures for a night but joy comes in the morning."*
> *"To whom much is given, much is required."*
> *"God won't give you more than you can bear."*

Honestly, I appreciate their sympathetic heart that desires to encourage me, but sometimes I feel like if just one more person hits me with one of those tired phrases, my face will turn fire engine red and the smoke and whistle will fly out of my ears until finally my head just explodes. Inevitably, the clichés come and go and I think to myself:

"Don't you think I've tried that one? Apparently I've built up an immunity to it at this point. It doesn't work on me anymore. Give me something new."

Even as I write that phrase I can hear God saying, "I've got plenty of fresh Word to encourage you, but you reduced your intake, remember?"... Holy... Shrimp. That hurts.

Today God is asking us to surrender to the shedding. What does that mean?! It means, being okay with not being okay for a while. It means being okay with being uncomfortable for a while. It means commanding your soul to do what you don't want to: stay in fellowship and remain accountable, stay in the Word, don't reduce your time in God's presence, increase it! If you really wanna move from Padawan to Jedi Knight[20,] then command yourself to encourage someone else even while you're still in process. Nothing says, "I trust God's Word," quite like giving

---

[20] Star Wars movie reference. A Padawan is a learner or apprentice, a Jedi is what Padawans are working to become.

the very thing you need, knowing that God will not let you go without it. I know you're probably wondering how you can be sure. His Word says so in Philippians 4:19. Everything you need, He will supply – period.

Will you surrender to the shedding today? Shedding doesn't feel good, but it also doesn't last always and it always marks a momentous occasion – your growth and graduation from one season to the next. Accept it. Surrender to it and watch God meet you in the process.

Sincerely,
In Pursuit of Surrender

Reflection Questions

As the above heading suggests, these questions are not meant to be breezed through. Rather, take your time and reflect. Speak to God and ask Him to reveal the things hiding in your heart so that you can answer these questions honestly and then submit your findings back to God. Also, after you've answered these questions, share them with your accountability partner so that you all can walk through this process together and they can hold you accountable regarding what you've shared. Lastly, there are just a few questions listed here. *To see the full set of reflection questions, turn to page 43 in your IPoS Journal.*

Are you currently in a shedding season?
Yes ☐ No ☐

If so, what things/people/places is God calling you to let go of?

If not, have you gone through such a season before? If so, reflect on your most recent shedding to answer the remaining questions.

"I would've really blown your mind with a wise quote here,
...but I forgot." *shrugs*

Surrendering To Selective Memory
(5/8/17)

I know, I know; when you read that heading you were thinking, "What the ham and crackers, Ange?! You're just making stuff up now! God did not tell you to write that." But, just give me a few moments and you'll understand what He means.

When I was a kid and my mom asked me to do certain chores (specifically, dishes... *shudders*), she would come back later to ensure that I had been obedient. Normally there would be at least one thing I hadn't done (probably the dishes. 'Cause, did I mention that I hate doing dishes? *shudders twice* I digress). When my mother inevitably asked why I hadn't completed the assigned task, the first excuse that would always come to my mind and escape my lips was, "... I forgot."

For those of you who are parents reading this, your left eye probably started involuntarily twitching when you read that because you immediately flashed back to the infuriating moment when you first heard that sorry excuse from your child(ren). It's okay, snap out of it and come back to us. For others reading this, perhaps someone forgot your birthday or your graduation day or Administrative Professionals' Day or Grandparents' Day or International Donut Day... Seriously, I could do this all day.

The point is, we've probably all encountered these moments in our lives when we've forgotten things or others have forgotten things they were supposed to do for us. It normally doesn't feel good. Indeed, depending on which side of the forgetfulness you're on you either feel guilty or insignificant. You see, because when we forget or are forgotten we attribute it to unintentionality in thought toward a person, thing or event. That is to say that because we were not intentional in commemorating that person, thing or event in our minds, it slipped out of our conscious thought and into obscurity somewhere between a subconscious awareness and total loss. Let's face it, whatever you forgot this time is sitting on a beach somewhere on the Sea of Obscurity sipping Mai Tais with the list of items you actually intended to buy at Target but kept forgetting (Doggone Target... It's so pretty and distracting. I digress.).

We've come to view forgetfulness as a passive phenomenon that is the result of unintentionality in the handling of our conscious thoughts. While there is truth to that definition, that's not the definition that God is calling us to understand today.

"... to *choose* **what I can't see,**

spoken **by a God**

that I can't see over

what I've already seen

from people I see every day

is a major struggle . . ."

The forgetfulness He wants us to surrender to today is quite the opposite. In Isaiah 43:18 God says to us, "Forget the former things; do not dwell on the past…" God is calling for an intentional forgetting.

Now, you may be thinking, "How can I be intentionally unintentional in handling a thought?"

Well, the answer is simple to say but a little more difficult to do:… Make a choice. A better translation of "forget" in this scripture is, "do not call to mind." The funny thing about this is that it doesn't work to tell yourself, "Okay, I'm just not going to think about 'fill in the blank,'" because, in saying that we're not going to think about it, we've already thought about it. In this case, what God is telling us to forget is *insert drum roll*… the past.

I'll be transparent in sharing that, as of late, this is my most difficult struggle—choosing faith over experience (choosing what I can't see, over what I've already seen). In fact, to choose what I can't see, spoken by a God that I can't see over what I've already seen from people I see every day is a major struggle for me.

You see, I believe God. I believe He is; that is to say, that He exists. I believe that His Word is true. But, what the enemy has been successful in convincing me of is that God's Word isn't true all of the time. The enemy has convinced me to believe that God's Word and His promises are true for everyone…

except me. You may be wondering how satan convinced me of such a thing. He's been so successful in his deception because he uses facts.

These are a few of the facts of my past and what the enemy used to convince me:

- I was born as, what society would call, a marginally pretty, black girl in a country that hates black people.
- I was born into, and raised in poverty (in the richest nation in the world).
- The fact is I was molested as a child by an extended, blood family member.
- I've been rejected more times than I can count, in situations ranging from relational to professional.
- I almost died at the age of fifteen.
- I was perennially the little shy girl who was overlooked.
- I was raised with an extended family that perpetuated double standards, confusion, jealousy and unhealthy competition.

In my mind, if God's Word is true and His promises are true, how could His promises and my life experience mutually exist? Therefore, the truth must be that God's promises are true for everyone except me; right? He's a crafty one, that satan; but,

God is wiser. Progressively, God has been revealing the lies that I bought that fuel this struggle between faith and experience. Perhaps you're fighting this battle too.

"God, how can your plans be for my good if all of these bad and harmful things have happened or keep happening to me?" But God says that all things work together for the good of those who love Him and are called according to His purpose[21] He says that what's happened to you or what has happened in your life and my life is exactly that: what happened. It is not what is happening. You see, God's Word is true, even for me, and His Word says in Isaiah 43:19 that He is doing a new thing. The reason why I couldn't perceive it and believe it until now was that I kept neglecting the premise in verse eighteen. I have refused to forget the past. Instead of not calling the past to mind, I called it to mind every chance I got. God would remind me of a promise He'd made toward me, yet I'd respond, "Yeah, but remember when...?"

Every time He spoke blessing over me, I'd remind Him of the pain and injustice of my past. If I'm going to accept and fully walk in all God is speaking over me in this new season, then I have to forget the past before I can see that He's doing a new thing.

---

[21] *Romans 8:28*

Therefore, today, and every day, I choose to not recall the hurts, fears and lies of the past. I recognize that I've got to replace those thoughts with other thoughts: whatsoever things are true, noble, right, pure, lovely, admirable, excellent and praiseworthy[22]. But, the great thing about God's Word is that it's true. Once I make the choice to forget the past, I'll have the ability to see the new thing that God is doing. All of those jaded memories from my past will be replaced with hope for the promised future. When I do this regularly, faith wins over experience every time.

Sincerely,
In Pursuit of Surrender

---

[22] *Philippians 4:8*

"...but my heart feels like it's time for God to pay up for all of the faithfulness I've been 'so graciously' dishing out."

Surrendering My Fallacy
(5/9/17)

"How long? How long must I call for help, but you do not listen? Or cry out to you... but you do not save?[23]"

These might as well have been my words, but they actually belonged to the Prophet, Habakkuk. They certainly express my thoughts, though. With every day that passes, with every day that sees me trying to honor God but still not seeing the manifestation of His promises, my sighs get longer and deeper and my faith and hope grow more and more faint. I hear myself crying out to God internally, "I'm doing my best. I am earnestly trying to honor you with my life, my thoughts, my words, my actions, my everything, and still more of the same?"

But, then I stop to think about what I've just said to God and what it implies. It occurs to me that as I analyze my complaint to God, a startling truth is unearthed... I still think that God owes me

---

[23] *Habakkuk 1:2*

something. Don't look at me like that! Of course I love God, but this could happen to any of us if we're not careful. I know that I owe God everything because:

1) He created me,
2) He breathes life into me every day and
3) Calvary.

Yet, there's a huge difference between head knowledge and heart knowledge. My head knows that I owe God absolutely all of me; but my heart feels like it's time for God to pay up for all of the faithfulness I've been "so graciously" dishing out.

Holy ham and crackers, Cletus! I make my doggone self sick! Did I just say that?!... Yeah, I did. I've not been quite suicidal enough to actually say that to God; but I'll be doggone if I haven't been saying it with my actions — with my complaints! I have been subconsciously living as though God's blessings and promises are what I deserve, what I'm owed for being faithful; but, that's so wrong on so many levels. I've got it all twisted. My faithfulness is what I owe to God because of His love and grace. Make no mistake, there's nothing I could ever say or do to deserve God's blessings and promises. In fact, even His offering of blessings and promises is the result of His love and grace.

How could I have possibly fallen subject to such a blatant fallacy, you ask? Simple. Fear and emotions make foolishness seem like truth. Because, fear invited itself in and whispered something like, "Is He just gonna leave you here forever? Doesn't He know how much this hurts? This is gonna be the rest of your life."

Then fear invited emotion to the party, at my house, mind you—an unsanctioned party—and emotion started running around and screaming frantically, "How could He do this to you?! If he loved you like He said, He would deliver you!!! You don't wanna die here, do you?! You're gonna die here! How could He let you die here?!?!" . . . Aaaaaaaand scene.

I'm not proud of it, but there you have it. But, before it gets too judgey in here, let's be honest, if enough people scream fire and flee from the movie theater, in an act of self-preservation, eventually you'll get up and run too; whether you see smoke or not. Fear and emotion have been whispering and screaming in my ears for a long while, so I fell for their act, hook, line and sinker. What they were really after was my faith and they did a number on it. I mean, honey, they tap danced all over my faith like their names were "Bo" and "Jangles"!

Fear and emotion know that they don't move God, faith does. We cry out to God, literally and figuratively, hoping that our tears will move Him. We run down every "what if" that fear whispers to us, and we expect God to be moved by our fearful arguments. In case you missed it, FAITH moves God. When we put our faith in God's Word enough to stand on it in the face of the storm —enough to step out on it when there's nothing else holding us up — that moves God. For those just tuning in to this broadcast, I have breaking news…

FAITH. MOVES. GOD. Period.

For those of you who drank the Kool-Aid right along with me (you know you drank it), for those who believed the fallacies that God owes us for our faithfulness and that if we whined and complaind enough, God would just pull us out of the fire, to you all, I offer a choice. I offer the same choice God has offered me: lies or truth. I don't know about you, but, lying to me is a huge pet peeve of mine.

> *"I choose to believe every word He's spoken . . ."*

I'm tired of being lied to. Even more than that, I'm tired of buying the lies. Today I choose to surrender the fallacies I've bought. I choose faith. I choose to remember that God doesn't owe me anything and that everything He offers is the result of His love and grace. I choose to believe every word He's spoken to me; I choose to believe what I can't see so that at the appointed time, no matter how long it takes, I will see what I've believed!

Sincerely,
In Pursuit of Surrender

"...it requires the humility to admit that I don't know everything and, specifically, that I don't know what's best for me."

Surrendering My Plans
(5/16/17)

Of all the things God has asked me to surrender thus far on this journey, this is one of the hardest. It's hardest, I think, because it requires the humility to admit that I don't know everything and, specifically, that I don't know what's best for me. Hardest, I think, because it requires the humility to give up control over some of the most intimate details of my life. Difficult is an understatement. Indeed it's taken many years to finally realize that I actually haven't given God control of the things I thought I had. It's unsettling and gives me a sinking feeling in the pit of my stomach to think that I thought I had surrendered all. For years, I believed I had, only to realize that I never had, or if I had, it was momentary and then I picked my will back up again.

Today I came to realize that I've been fighting God's will for singlehood in my life because I was afraid that admitting that He called me to singlehood right now meant that I was acknowledging that I would be single forever. Today, God showed me how tightly I'd been holding onto the desire to choose my own mate based on what finite information I had. I had chosen to limit God based on my limitations and in doing so I limited God's blessing in my life. As it stands, if God were to present me to the right one right now, I might dismiss him because he wasn't who or what I thought he should be. I might even be tempted to be disappointed with God's choice because... "my choice was better."

Looks around for lightning bolts... Funny story, I'm writing this in a rainstorm.

But, isn't that what I tell God every time I refuse to surrender all?

"God, I surrender everything except for the plans I've worked out that are actually better than the ones you've worked out and haven't shown me yet."

I'm laughing even as I write that statement because it makes me think about someone inviting us to do something we don't really want to do, so we say we're unavailable and they're like, "but I didn't say when it was." But, that is exactly what I've been saying to God. "Oh no; I'm not available for that."

Then God is like, "But I haven't even told you what it is yet."

And in reply, I say, "Yeah, but I'm still unavailable because it's not what I have planned out."

Today is the day that God made me aware of my tendency to "false surrender;" therefore, today I choose to truly surrender my plans for His because, let's face it, His ways are higher than mine. His thoughts are higher than mine[24]. And His plans are better than mine. Today, I surrender all of my plans to Him and I'm not picking them back up...

Sincerely,
In Pursuit of Surrender

P.S.- If, by chance, you see me walking around with my own plans back in my hands SLAP THEM OUT! 'Kay?! Great! Bye!

Withholding Something
(5/16/19)

Hey! You know that AMAZING song by Pastor William McDowell?! I know, you're like, "Which one, Ange. They're all amazing!" My bad; let me be more specific.(I'll say it again for the people in the back, "SPECIFIC," not "PACIFIC." ...That's an ocean. I digress.) The song I'm thinking of is "Withholding Nothing." Isn't that an amazingly wonderful song?... Until you actually have to do it. It can be hard to offer God every part of us, withholding nothing. Truly, it is difficult. I mean, even when we want to, our flesh is

---

[24] *Isaiah 55:8-9*

so fickle and covert that sometimes it picks back up what we had every intention of leaving at the feet of Jesus before we even realize what's happened.

The next thing we know, we're walking around carrying all of the weight that we left at His feet just a few weeks ago, and then some! So, let's talk honestly about it. What are some areas of your life that you've surrendered to God or thought you'd surrendered but realized that they had a bungee cord attached to them and just bounced right back to you? What are those areas of your life that you are still not ready and wanting to surrender to Him? Why don't we take some time in our journals and prayer time today to ask God to Psalm 139 us. (Yes, I made "Psalm 139" a verb... 'Cause, who gon' check me?).

I digress. Using Psalm 139: 23-24 as a guide, let's ask God to not just search our hearts, but to reveal to us the truth of what is hidden in our hearts; if it's hiding from us, it's definitely trying to hide from Him. Let's ask God to show us the areas of our lives that we've been withholding out of fear, anxiety, shame, pride, whatever! Then, when He's revealed them, I strongly encourage you to begin the process of surrender. Maybe for you that looks like telling God that you truly want to surrender those areas, but you're not sure how to take your hands off of them or telling Him that you want to surrender those areas but need the courage to do it. Maybe that looks like telling Him that you still aren't ready to surrender that area, but you desire to get to the place where you are. Everyone is at a different place and that's okay.

No one's gonna judge you for where you are. All that matters is that there is a willingness to surrender all to God, even if that means you desire to **have** the desire to surrender all (no, that's not a typo), but you recognize you're not there yet. God can handle the truth, whatever it may be. The change that we're seeking comes in the uncomfortable moments; so, let's spend some time journaling, praying and speaking with our accountability partners about those areas that we've been withholding. Surrender's gotta start somewhere. Let's go!

Sincerely,
In Pursuit of Surrender

"I've been carrying around the weight of a responsibility that isn't even mine. It's God's, no less!"

Surrendering The Weight
(5/23/17)

"Somebody's breakthrough depends on your obedience." Has anyone ever said those words or something similar to you? Yeah; me too. Recently I realized that those words that were meant to motivate me actually became baggage. Subconsciously, I've been carrying around the weight of other people's breakthroughs; and while it's true that there are people that God has assigned to me, I allowed the weight of that truth to somehow displace the truths that God has extended a standing offer to carry my yoke. Some plant and some water but God is the one who brings the increase.

I've been carrying around the weight of a responsibility that isn't even mine. It's God's, no less!

Let me make this clear. I still have the responsibility of walking in obedience to God's calling on my life, but, that's where the responsibility shifts. Once I operate in obedience to God, He is the one who then uses that obedience to touch the hearts of those He's assigned to me.

Think of your calling as a baby. When we have babies, we have them dedicated before God and our family and friends, right? Now, there are many ways this is done, but the point is that we are in the practice of offering our blessing — in the form of a tiny, perfect human being — back to God. It is no different with our gifts and calling. When we learn our gifts and calling it is our responsibility to offer them back to God.

When we offer ourselves as living sacrifices[25,] it means that we also offer our gifts, talents, passions and purpose to God. Why? Because we can't do, with those things, what God can. If I can sing well and decide I'm going to sing for my own pleasure and profit (my own glory), then I might become a one-hit wonder. Or worse yet, a "successful" music artist with all of the fame, money and material things I could want, but still be empty and unfulfilled. Why? Because God doesn't place those things inside of us for us; nor are they meant to be used apart from God's Spirit, through which they've been given to us. That's like unplugging your laptop from the outlet and expecting it to remain powered indefinitely. That's not how our gifts, passions, and purpose work. In fact, that's not how we work! At some point, we shut down, we run out of juice, we break down, we stop working because we weren't meant to operate away from our power source. We weren't meant to

---

[25] *Romans 12:1*

carry that weight. We were made to offer ourselves —
including all of our gifts, passions and purpose — back
to God.

Today, I gratefully lay down the weight of
bringing the increase, because, that is not in my job
description. Today, I choose to offer all of me as a
living sacrifice and do what God has asked me to do.
Then I'll leave the work of breakthrough, deliverance,
heart change and life change to the Holy Spirit. That's
exactly where that responsibility belongs, on the
shoulders of the one who can handle it. Today I
choose to avoid the burnout and depression that
comes from taking on and carrying what I wasn't
made to carry. I choose to lay aside the weight that
Paul talks about in Hebrews 12:1 because I intend to
run this race with longevity. I'm in this for the long
game, so today I choose to leave this baggage behind.

Sincerely,
In Pursuit of Surrender

"Waiting is a part of the process.
It's what we do in the wait that counts."

Surrendering Impatience
(5/30/17)

I have a sneaking suspicion that this will not be the last time we talk about waiting or waiting well. In case you can't tell, that's kind of where God has me… in the waiting room; and that's by design. It is not by happenstance that the last several of my seasons have been waiting seasons. Difficult phases of waiting. Gestation… Yeah, that's it! In retrospect, I've been going through gestational phases.

As I get older, more and more of my peers are having children; and it's always pretty interesting to watch the progression of emotions throughout the pregnancies. It normally starts full of excitement to meet their little one. Then, they're overjoyed to meet their little one… and they're getting tired. Then, they can't wait to meet the little one… and get their bladder back. Then, they're so excited to meet their little one… and find a comfortable sleeping position again. Finally, once the due date has come and gone, the eviction notices are posted all over social media.

"Okay, I know you want to take your good 'ole time, but mommy and daddy are ready for you to get here NOW!... and I can't wait to see your sweet face... But mostly, just get out now!"

I have to laugh because that's exactly where I am right now. God has been gracious enough to give me a glimpse of the destiny He's prepared for me and I'm so excited, "I can't wait to meet you, destiny! I'm so blessed and I'm counting down the days!"

"I finally understand why

Sarah laughed."

Then, somewhere during that excitement, the days grew longer and far more than I expected. I was still excited, but now a little uncomfortable because what I was expecting by this time — the joy of walking in these new blessings — was not what I was experiencing. Days turned into weeks, turned into months, turned into a year, turned into several years and... I finally understand why Sarah laughed.

God was reiterating a promise to Abraham that had yet to come to pass. I can hear Sarah's scoffing chortle in my cynical laugh as, once again, God confirms everything He's spoken over these last several years is true and is nearing. *insert cynical chortle* "Yeah, okay. I've heard that before, God."

Sarah gets a bum rap for her lack of faith; but the truth of the matter is, we, if we're honest, have probably all been in the same place at least once and it likely didn't take us more than a decade to get there.

Just like those soon-to-be mamas, we are ready to get past the discomfort and get to the joy of the blessing. However, just like every day in the womb has a point to the end of preparing a baby for birth and life outside the womb, every day that we wait is designed to prepare us for a life of destiny. I know, I know! I wish I had better news for you, but the truth is that learning to wait well is just a necessary part of our journey. I mean, if Jesus had to wait, why wouldn't we?

Can you imagine the moments leading up to Christ's death? They were agonizing. He sat in the garden praying. He had carried this baby to full term. He anxiously awaited the glory that was to come, but first he had to get through the horrifying labor of...

an unwanted arrest — *waiting*
a relentless physical beating — *waiting*

a shameful walk — *waiting*
a painful nailing — *waiting*
an agonizing hanging — *waiting*
an excruciating separation — *waiting*
a cursed death — *waiting*
a borrowed tomb — *waiting*
a silent graveyard — *waiting*
a weekend in hell — *waiting*

and finally a majestic rising! Destiny!

If Jesus had to wait through that, I think you and I can wait through this. Whatever your "this" is, if God has asked you to wait, resolve to wait patiently. Resolve to wait well.

The fruit of the Spirit is love, joy, peace, patience[26]… That Spirit dwells in each of us that have accepted Christ as our Savior; and patience is the fruit it produces in us and from us. So, let's make a choice today to let the Holy Spirit do its work. Today, I choose to surrender to the Holy Spirit who works patience in me. I choose to surrender my impatience and trust God's perfect *kairos* (appointed time).

Sincerely,
In Pursuit of Surrender

---

[26] *Galatians 5:22*

Teamwork Makes the Dream Work
(5/19/2019)

"Teamwork makes the dream work" is a phrase that we, the staff of Macedonia, very often verbalize and put to work. We strive to operate as a team and support each other to make sure the work gets done. It doesn't matter what anyone's official title is, only that there is a need to be filled; if there's a need for a clean-up crew, then we become the clean-up crew. If the need is for a server, then consider your ministry guests served. We recognize that, just like we are not called to do ministry alone, we are not called to do life alone either; therefore, accountability is a very highly held value at Macedonia. Accountability is not only expected in our work, but also in our personal lives.

Why did I just go into that long spiel about accountability? Well, because, remember that accountability is a key component of our surrender process. James 5:16 says, "Therefore confess your sins to each other and pray for each other so that you may be healed. The prayer of a righteous person is powerful and effective." This verse falls in a stretch of verses that are discussing the power of prayer.

If our accountability partners are going to hold us accountable, then they need to know the 4-1-1 (for those of you born after 1990, 4-1-1 means "information"). This verse in James explains one of the reasons why an accountability relationship must be a non-judgmental space with someone who is invested in your spiritual growth and journey of overcoming. It's imperative because there will be times when we need to confess our sins to someone who can lift us in prayer so that we don't stay in that sin-place. We need a non-judgmental place to share the struggles that perhaps led us to that sin-place.

Perhaps the sin is that we initiated a romantic relationship and crossed boundaries that we knew we shouldn't, but that relationship started because God asked us to wait for His best and we got impatient in the wait. Maybe the sin is that we disrespect our boss on the job as often as we can[27], but the sin started because we didn't stay at the job God asked us to stay at because we wanted a raise and more power; so we got impatient and ended up at a job that God never called us to. Think about those areas where you've become impatient with God. Has that impatience led you to a sin place? Even if it hasn't, it's important to confess your frustrations with God and His timing before those feelings carry you off to a sin-place.

Today we're going to spend time with our accountability partner in God's presence. This person is a safe space (if not, then you either do not have the right accountability partner or you all need to re-

[27] Yes, this is a sin. See Rom. 13:1-2, Titus 3:1-2... You get the idea

discuss the dynamics of your accountability relationship). Within the protection of that safe space, confess areas where you've grown impatient with God.

Confess where you ended up in that sin-place; but also confess those areas that you just contemplated going to a sin-place, because an uninterrupted thought very easily becomes an action. Interrupt the thought! Confess it! Put it into the light.

The enemy doesn't operate in the light, he can't; it's not his domain. So, when you choose to put these thoughts in the light, you take away his power and give God permission to have His way in that area. Let's break out our journals and begin sharing the 4-1-1 with our accountability partners. Then, we'll spend time in prayer together as we surrender our impatience (and the places it's led us) to God.

Sincerely,
In Pursuit of Surrender

"God is still faithful... Even on grocery days."

Surrendering In My Singlehood
(6/10/17)

Grocery days and travel days are always the hardest. I don't know why it comes so clearly on those days but that's when I feel the weight of my singlehood most. I've got a theory though. I don't talk about being single much. I don't discuss it because when I do, it's very easy for me to get frustrated. In fact, I'm willing to bet that nine out of ten conversations about singlehood will end in me being frustrated or angry. I hate talking about singlehood because someone usually feels the need to offer advice like:

"He'll come when you're not looking," or
"He'll come when you're not even thinking about it,"

or

"Enjoy this time while you can; marriage ain't all roses and chocolate."

insert the most side-eyed side-eye EVER

On behalf of single people everywhere, this "advice" is not helpful, especially because it's normally coming from those who are single and don't want a relationship/marriage or those who are already married. The number one reason, however, that I hate talking about my singlehood is that I almost always feel like my discontentment with being single is an indication that I'm a bad Christian or immature in my faith. People who aren't feeling the weight of singlehood can so unwittingly make you feel guilty about something that is so natural. It's not that they intend to, more often than not they actually don't intend it; but inevitably, they say something that causes me to wonder if my desire for a God-honoring relationship and marriage in this season makes me spiritually immature or lacking in faith.

For all of my single brothers and sisters who desire a God-honoring relationship and marriage, there is nothing wrong with you. There is nothing wrong with us. Everyone has had that one thing that they wanted, but just outside of God's timing. There is nothing wrong with desiring things; the key is to remain submitted to God's will anyhow.

When we, like Rebekah and Jacob in Genesis 27, try to take matters into our own hands to make God's will happen, it's a sure sign that either what we thought was God's will is not or it is God's will but not His timing. The truth is, whatever God has spoken, He will bring it to pass. He may ask us to participate in the process, but He is the one who has a plan for our lives and He is the one who is working that plan. Our end of the deal is to remain submitted in the process. I'm sure you're thinking, "What the heck does that mean, Ange?"

"I will not try to

manipulate

my circumstances to make them

"look like"

what God spoke."

It means that I may not be enjoying singlehood right now, but I'm still open to receive what God is teaching me in my single season. It means, I may not like being single right now, but you won't find me out hunting for a man because that's not what God has called me to do; He's called me to wait—to remain where He has positioned me. It means, I will not try to manipulate my circumstances to make them "look like" what God spoke. For me, God has asked me to wait. God has impressed upon me that when He presents me to my husband, he (my husband) will find me about my Father's business. He will find me walking in purpose and anointing.

So, for all my single people desiring a God-honoring relationship and marriage, keep ya head up. Know that it's okay to feel that longing, but don't let it be the greatest longing in your heart. And when these natural feelings arise, lest you become overwhelmed, surrender them to God. He's the one who knows what to do with them.

Earlier I said I had a theory on why grocery and travel days are the hardest for me. My theory is that I feel this longing so strongly on those days because of what they represent. Grocery days with Mom always require time, effort and a decent bit of physical exertion. You see, we walk all over Sam's Club and Walmart (always in that order. You don't deviate from Mama's plan. Mama wants Sam's then Wally World? Mama gets Sam's then Wally World. Period). While Mom grabs what she needs, I'm calculating in my head and calling out totals so she knows where she stands in her food budget. Once that's done the real work begins. I lug all of those groceries from my car up the twenty-three steps to her apartment— Up and down, up and down, each time a little more winded than the last. Finally, once all is unloaded, I collapse into my car, blast the AC and fight the urge to cry. Why? Because I wish I had help. Not just someone willing to help, but someone who intentionally comes alongside me to help because they want to. Not because they were asked to, but because they've covenanted to.

Have you figured out that I'm not just talking about groceries? Yes, it would be wonderful to have a nice, strong, handsome brotha (Hallelujah!) walk up and down those steps with me to carry the load; but more than that, I want someone to walk through life's ups and downs with me, not because I've asked him to but because he's chosen to, because he wants to. You know what's great about that? I, in turn, get to walk through life's ups and downs with him, not because he asks me to, but because I choose to, I've covenanted to… Because I want to.

The theory continues that travel days are so difficult because I love to travel. I love the freedom, adventure, joy, beauty, peace and catharsis of travel; however, as I set out to travel, whether a road trip, air travel or whatever, the moment comes when I desire to share the experience with him (whomever he is. Lol). Let's face it, when we really love something, we normally want to share it with someone. Not everyone, but someone. I long to experience the adventures and joys of life with him; and I'm honest and wise enough to admit that some of those trips might be filled with awkward silence because we had a disagreement just before we left home, but with the right one, that awkward silence doesn't stand a chance. Now, please notice that the grocery trips and traveling don't stop. All my singles, please don't put your life, calling or ministry on hold waiting for the right one. Keep experiencing life in the now. It's okay to feel whatever emotions you need to feel; but surrender them to God and keep living!!!

So, that's the theory—these days are so difficult for me because of what they represent. The truth is, though, that no matter how I feel, I trust God. Therefore, I give my feelings a little room to breathe, but then I submit them to God because, let's face it, our soulish feelings can't be trusted.

Today, I choose to surrender all of my feelings to God as He patiently walks me through my single season because... today was a grocery day, and grocery days are always the hardest. But, God is still faithful... even on grocery days.

Sincerely,
In Pursuit of Surrender

Growth
(5/20/19)

Thank God for growth. It was difficult to re-read that last chapter—seeing my raw emotions on the page as I prepared to write this follow-up. In truth, for a fleeting moment, I wanted to edit and censor some of that truth. For a brief sliver of a moment, I thought to myself, "Wow, folks are really gonna think..." and then I responded to myself,

"No. What's written there was the truth and people need the truth. No more watered down and censored iterations of the truth, just the pure, unadulterated, un-finessed truth. People need to know that if that's where they are, that's okay because it won't always be that way; it's just a checkpoint in the process and it does not define them. People need to know that they are not the only ones who are or have been in that place."

Therefore, the truth remains uncensored and because it remains uncensored, I get the joy of seeing the growth that God has worked in me in the last two years. Are there still difficult days? Absolutely. The point is, I'm at a much better place in my singlehood because God has given me perspective and wisdom and it's made all the difference.

One of the reasons why many of us struggle with singlehood is because of how we've been taught. I don't believe this was an intentional teaching, but we were taught, nonetheless. We've grown up in a culture that deifies relationships and bastardized understandings of love. For those of us who grew up in church, the chances are that nine times out of ten we didn't get to escape that cultural deification. You would think that because the church is to be set apart and not look like the world, we would escape the not-so-subliminal messaging of relational deification, but nope, not at all. You see, in the church it's not just relationship, but marriage that has been deified. Again, this has not been the intention, but it has become the message.

It's not hard to find a married couples ministry at church, or a married couples retreat, or a married couples workshop, conference, seminar, you name it. You know what's harder? Finding a healthy singles' ministry in a church.

"That's not true! We have a singles' ministry at my church, Ange!"

That's nice, but is it a healthy singles' ministry? What do I mean by healthy? Well, for starters, whenever there's a singles' ministry event, does it normally turn out to be marriage prep or are the singles being taught how to thrive in and successfully navigate Christian singlehood? Are singles being told what to expect in marriage and how to "become ready" for marriage or are they being told that there is nothing wrong with being single — that there's purpose in being single in Christ? Are singles being told the truth that they have power in the Kingdom because they can serve the Lord unencumbered?

Normally there are two options when it comes to singles' ministries in churches: there is no ministry or the ministry is essentially a marriage prep ministry/hook-up spot. It's the "Lite" version of the married couples ministry. You know, "Let's inundate the singles with images of happily married couples and information about what it takes to become a happily married couple; but let's not set them up to thrive well in the season they are currently called to."

I get it. I recognize that healthy marriages should absolutely be a priority in any church, but that should be a priority, not the priority. What happens — when we spend all our time telling singles how to prepare for marriage — is that we subliminally communicate that marriage is the goal and not God. Then we, singles, spend our time longing for marital relationship with another person instead of relationship with God. What happens is that oftentimes singles spend all of our time praying and hoping and looking for the right one instead of seeking first His Kingdom and righteousness and letting all other things be added unto us[28]. What happens is that singles are unintentionally fed this lie

---

[28] *Matthew 6:33*

that marriage is better than singlehood, that serving God cannot be effectively done unless and until you are married. But, that's a lie from the pit of hell!

You really want to know what's better, marriage or singlehood? It's… whichever God has called you to in that season! That's it! One is not inherently "better than" the other! Whether you are single or married, the focus should always be God; and we've lost sight of that. We've been unintentionally taught to glorify marriage, not God. But, that time is done. It's time to restore God to His throne in our lives and it starts by breaking through the generational fallacy that marriage equals holiness. IT. DOES. NOT.

So, for my fellow single brothers and sisters that have been running around feeling like you are broken and that's why you aren't married yet, feeling like you are a second class citizen in the Kingdom of God because you don't have a boo, bae, baby, honey — hear me loud and clear when I say that marriage does not make us whole. God does. There is nothing wrong with you. God is not punishing you. You are not irreparably broken and unworthy of marital love. You are not half a Christian. You are not on Heaven's practice squad hoping to earn your spot on the team. You have a powerful position in the Kingdom of God, and you have the ability to do some things that married folks cannot do as easily or at all. You have the ability to GO where God calls you, unencumbered. You have the ability to do mighty work in advancing The Kingdom. I know that we've been unintentionally conditioned to believe the lies, but here is the truth—we are not at a disadvantage because we are single! The enemy has stolen the joy of singlehood from us, shifting the paradigm of holiness from chasing God to chasing marriage. But today, we take back the joy of our singlehood! We know the truth now, the question is, what will we do with it?

I want to tell you a story; sometime last year I was invited to minister in song at a wedding. I was excited to accept and arrived at the church about an hour early on the day of the wedding. There was one other woman, a pastor, ministering in song as well and we were both led to the choir loft in the sanctuary to await the start of the nuptial festivities. I didn't know this woman, and she didn't know me; she was a little older than me—from my parents' generation. As we sat there, we were mostly quiet, taking in the beauty of the atmosphere, with some brief spurts of conversation.

Finally, this woman turned to me and curiously inquired, "Are you married?"

"No, ma'am," I answered.

"Oh, well, we gon' have to get you married," she exclaimed enthusiastically.

Mind you, I don't know this woman. I only knew the few bits of information we had shared in the moments prior to this one. I digress. I respectfully, yet non-chalantly responded something like,

"Oh, no; God will send him at the right time."

"Oh! That's right! You're right!" she back-tracked. I smiled inside. It was a brief moment, but quite freeing. That woman meant no harm, and I certainly held no ill-will nor hurt feelings during and in the time since that encounter. She was, in truth, very sweet and I enjoyed her company that day.

I emerged from that moment stronger and wiser, having faced the lie head on, no longer buying into the fallacy that marriage is better than singlehood. There was not a moment of doubt as we exchanged brief dialogue. There was only a confidence that I possessed the truth and could no longer be swayed to give into the lie. I am not "less than." I am not damaged goods. I am not cursed. I am actually blessed, purposed and positioned to be used by God! I have power, and so do you!

In case no one's told you, you now know the truth about your singlehood. The question is, what will you do with the truth? Will you continue to allow the enemy to incite you to despair and discontentment or will you armor-up and look the lie in the face and speak the truth?

I choose to speak truth to power; after all, we aren't fighting against flesh and blood; we're fighting against principalities[29]. I choose to recognize that we are not in a battle against married folks; we are in a battle against the enemy that would try to continue the generational lie that single is bad. I declare that this is the generation where that lie comes to die. No more giving voice to it. I only have room in my mouth for the truth. I thank God for growth. I thank Him for truth, and I thank Him that He continues to teach me how to surrender my singlehood to Him and watch Him do more with it than I could ever imagine. What is your choice?

Sincerely,
In Pursuit of Surrender

---

[29] *Ephesians 6:12*

Reflection Questions

Whether you are single or married, I invite you to take a look at and answer these questions for yourself. Then, along with your point(s) of accountability, pray through your answers and ask God to break the stronghold of this lie in your life. Finally, ask God how He wants to use you to be a part of breaking this generational lie. *You can find the full set of Reflection Questions in your IPoS Journal on page 76*

For my single folks:

1. Have you ever felt like you were single because something was wrong with you?
2. If you've ever felt like something was wrong with you and it contributed to your being single, can you identify an event, comment or conversation that precipitated that feeling?

For my married folks:

1. Do you believe that you maximized your time as a single person before you got married or do you believe that you may have rushed out of singleness before God was done shaping you there?

"We've bought the lie that time heals all wounds. That's hogwash and horse petooty!"

Surrendering My Brokenness, Part 1
(6/26/17)

As I introspect today, I realize that I've been withholding vital parts of myself from God and for a most peculiar reason. Do you remember when you were a kid and you were afraid of the dark? Do you remember that feeling you'd get when you knew the boogeyman had walked into the room even though you couldn't see him? Do you remember your eyes darting around the room trying to spot him in the pitch black; then, finally, in a panic, you'd pull the blanket up over your head? Your breathing, heavy as you held the blanket firmly above your head, but soon, relief washed over you and you drifted off to dreamland because you knew you were safe if he couldn't see you. No? That never happened to you?... Oh, well, that was me as a kid. If I could sprint across the dark room and just bury my whole body under my blanket, I knew I was safe; because, deep in the safety of my blanket, if I couldn't see the boogeyman, then he couldn't hurt me.

Sounds foolish now, (unless you still do that... In which case, no judgment here; carry on.) but at the time it seemed like pretty sound logic. You know what's more foolish than believing that as a kid? You guessed it, believing it as an adult. Now, granted, as adults we don't still believe in the boogeyman (unless, of course, you still do… in which case, still no judgment here; carry on); even so, we buy into that logic when it comes to our brokenness. We believe that if we just ignore our brokenness and turn a blind eye, it ceases to exist. We believe that if we put it out of our mind long enough, it will go away. It will heal itself. We've bought the lie that time heals all wounds. That's hogwash and horse petooty! It isn't true! Time without treatment does not heal wounds. Sometimes time causes infection. Sometimes it causes atrophy. Sometimes time causes things to fuse together and grow back improperly or it causes scar tissue that leaves us permanently disfigured. Time does not heal wounds; God does; but, more about that later.

"…this brokenness would break me."

What I'm realizing is that I've been hoping that refusing to acknowledge this brokenness would make it go away. I know there are things that God has in store in the coming season that require me to be whole in order to handle them — new relationships, new ministry opportunities, new business endeavors — and I've been hoping that if I just ignore this brokenness, that God would too.

Maybe if I turn a blind eye, God will let it slide just this once. God has healed some of my brokenness in the past; can't that healing be enough to get me to the next season? The answer is no because, even if I did walk into the next season with this brokenness, because of what I'm called to, I get the sense that this brokenness would break me.

You see, this brokenness is old. It's been around a long time. It's had time to form scar tissue. I've been dressing it up in cute clothes and accessories and walking around as if it doesn't exist, hoping that, by the time I got home, it would be gone somehow. When I get home, though, and take off all the trappings of beauty and look myself in the mirror, it's there starring back at me, big and bold as ever. It's tied to my self-esteem, but it's so much more than that...

But, before facing this brokenness head-on, today I choose to surrender it. I choose to surrender this brokenness by acknowledging that it exists. I acknowledge it to myself, and I acknowledge it to God. I choose to surrender to God all of this brokenness that I've been withholding. It's been buried all these years under masks and more recent brokenness; and little by little, God has been healing each layer. Diligently, God has been doing surgery and each surgery goes a little deeper. Now, He wants to heal the root of it all. My heart and spirit want to open up and receive new blessings that God promised, but, my hands are too crippled by the arthritis caused by clinging to this brokenness.

I now realize that I can't receive all that God has spoken over me until I allow Him to heal this brokenness. In this moment of clarity, God has healed the arthritis by making me aware of it and preparing my heart for this moment. My hands are now open, my heart is ready, all that's left is the surrender.

Sincerely,
In Pursuit of Surrender

P.S. - Part I is about identifying and acknowledging the area(s) of brokenness that God wants to heal. Let's spend some time in our journals. You may be aware of brokenness in your life, maybe not. Let's pray Psalm 139:23-24 again, asking God to show us ourselves, including those broken places that He desires to heal in this season. Once He reveals those areas, jot them down and let's continue on to Part II. Once we identify the brokenness we face, then the real work begins…

"Of all these scenarios, this is the one I should trust, but, 'should' and 'do' are two completely different words."

Surrendering My Brokenness, Part 2
(6/26/17)

So, what's the big deal? What's this stronghold that grandfathered its way into my life long before I knew how to fight it? As I said before, it's tied to my self-esteem, but it's not quite the same. The big, bad wolf is... the way I understand myself. *crickets* I mean, I wasn't expecting applause or anything, but really? Crickets, guys? Lol.

Some would argue that, the way I understand myself is exactly what self-esteem is. I'm not going to argue the point; I will, however, humbly submit that it is, instead, what self-esteem is based on; rooted in. But, they are not the same. For me, self-esteem is the way that I esteem or value myself based on my understanding of who I really am. I know you're probably thinking, "Well, what the heck does that mean, Ange—understanding who I really am?"

When I say that, I don't simply mean being aware of your personality style (introvert vs. extrovert) or your character traits (trustworthy, goofy, loyal, etc.). When I say, "understanding who I truly am," I mean understanding God's original design—His anointing in my life. That is to say, God's original intent when He created me. Who did God make me before the world abused, devalued, disrespected and forced its lies upon me? What was God's original intent when He spoke the name Angelique in Heaven, before it was released in the earth (pronounced: ON-juh-leek, to settle all discussion)?

If I showed a millennial a picture of a washboard, depending on their musical taste, they might say it was a musical instrument in folk and country music. Or, depending on their decorating sense, they might say it is a rustic traditionalist conversation piece. But, what they may not know is that the original purpose for a washboard was not music or decoration. It was created to meet a need. It was created for the purpose of washing clothes. If I set a jar of Play-Doh on a table and asked ten adult people what it was, they'd probably all say some variation of, "a kid's toy." The truth is, it was originally created as wallpaper cleaner. I kid you not! If I'm lying, I'm flying; and I assure you that my toesies are firmly planted on the ground.

I know, you're wondering what a washboard and Play-Doh have to do with brokenness and identity. Here it is, if I sat in a room full of people of all ages, races, nationalities, etc., what would they say I was created for? To make babies? To cook and clean all day? To be a sex toy for a man? Who would they say I was just by looking at me? A student, a mom, a slob, a whore, a saint? What would they say about me based on sight alone? I'm beautiful, ugly, marginally pretty, too fat, too thin, too dark, not dark enough, unkempt, too pristine?

What if people who actually knew me were all gathered in a room? Who would they say I am? Nice, rude, goofy, serious, pretty, homely, fashionable, trustworthy, not to be trusted, wishy-washy, bougie, down to earth, made to sing, made to write, made to counsel, made to entertain?

Now, suppose I sat in a room filled with God The Father, The Son and the Holy Spirit, what would they say about me? Who would they say I am? Of all these scenarios, this is the one I should trust, but, "should" and "do" are two completely different words. I've entrusted my identity to those who know me and those who don't; yet, the one I should trust to help me understand who I am is the one I haven't asked. It never even occurred to me to ask. I've asked about my purpose, I've asked about direction, but I don't think I've ever asked God who I am. I've asked Him to allow me to see me as He does; but I didn't even fully understand my request. Now I do.

God has made it abundantly clear that before I can walk into this new season, I have to know who I am. After Jesus was baptized, but before the wilderness and being launched into His earthly ministry, God publicly affirmed His identity. "This is my son whom

I love and in whom I am well pleased.[30]" Imagine that. Jesus hadn't even done ministry yet, but God cracked the sky and sent His Spirit down to affirm who Jesus was and that God was pleased with Him. Not based on what Jesus did or didn't do but based on who He was—God's son.

I often think of myself as a disgraced daughter, sort of like the prodigal son. I view myself as the marred and cracked clay pot[31.] But, what I know is that the prodigal son was received and treated as if his infraction never happened and the marred clay pot in the Master Potter's hands is re-formed for His glory. Yet, for some reason, even though I know these truths, I still view myself as marred and disgraced. The time for that is passed.

Today I choose to surrender this brokenness. I choose to surrender this illegitimate understanding of who I am—God's original intent in creating me. Today, I choose to lay aside the lies I've bought about who I am and how God sees me.

Sincerely,
In Pursuit of Surrender

---

[30] *Luke 3:22*
[31] *Jeremiah 18:4*

P.S.- *Before moving on to Part III, think through and answer each of the reflection questions in your IPoS Journal on page 84.*

Reflection Questions

Do you identify with this chapter?
Yes ☐ No☐ Why or why not?

Do you believe you know your identity (God's original design, who He's called you to be)?
Yes ☐ No☐

If yes, discuss your identity with your accountability partner/group. If no, have you ever asked God to show you your true identity?

"Throw me a frikken bone here!"
~Dr. Evil, Austin Powers: International Man of Mystery

Surrendering My Brokenness, Part 3
- The Reason
(6/26/17)

Remember in chapter sixteen when I mentioned a "most peculiar" reason why I had been trying to ignore this brokenness? Well, today's the day I tell all. I had been neglecting this brokenness because I felt that if I acknowledged it, it would take too long for God to heal. I felt like unearthing and opening this can of worms would send me on some sort of years-long spiral that would prolong the coming of this new season even more and as Ms. Sweet Brown so aptly conveyed, "ain't nobody got time fuh dat!" (go ahead, Google her, I'll wait) The problem with that logic is that it doesn't take into account God's sovereignty. God is not bound by our understanding of time.

All I knew was that I didn't want to be stuck in this waiting season for even more years, just awaiting God's promises. I was and am tired of waiting. I've been as faithful as I can to the process. I've been committed to not jumping out of the pot undone. I've sacrificed, killing my flesh by choosing praise and worship over my feelings. I've been intentional about choosing faith even when it's been challenged time and time again. I really am so ready for this waiting to be over, but, then God throws a monkey wrench in my plans. He very kindly told me that I have yet to see and understand myself as He does. I whined and complained, begging Him not to leave me here longer. I was crying for Him to just let me get to the next season and then He could show me the way He views me.

"You made promises and I've been faithful. You can't just leave me here again, please!"

But, I was begging and pleading about *chronos*, forgetting that God isn't bound by it. We observe *chronos* time — a sequential and quantifiable passing of time. God operates according to *kairos* time — the appointed or opportune time — and nothing can thwart the plan of God[32,] not even *chronos*. Because the God I serve is not confined by *chronos*, I am reminded that He can operate in acceleration if He so chooses. In fact, I'm reminded of a Word that He had spoken through my Pastor a season or two ago. He spoke about how He was going to work through the spirit of acceleration and I immediately grabbed that Word because who wouldn't want to see in months what would normally take years?! But, I misappropriated that Word. I thought it meant that I

---

[32] *Job 42:2, again*

was coming out of the storm — this season — in months…

Me: "Yes, Jesus!"

God: "No, Ange."

Me: "Aw, c'mon, Jesus!" Then I muttered in my best Dr. Evil voice, "Throw me a frikken bone here!"

"I thought I was

waiting on Him —

and impatiently, might I add —

but God was really

waiting patiently on me."

But what I didn't realize until this moment is that this was what God was referring to. This is the season where He moves through the spirit of acceleration. He was just waiting for me to get to the place where I was ready to surrender it to Him so that He could work this all out for His glory. Now, ain't that some mess?! I thought I was waiting on Him —

and impatiently, might I add — but God was really waiting patiently on me.

Today, I choose to shift my focus from all of the things I've been wanting, praying and hoping for to instead, focus on God's grace. I choose to focus on His favor, mercy and patience. I choose to surrender to His healing process for as long as it takes. I choose to remember that God is faithful even in all of my brokenness. Today, I choose to surrender. I'm asking God to show me who He created me to be — His original design. I'm asking Him to show me in His Word what He says about me and who He says I am.

Sincerely,
In Pursuit of Surrender

Stronger Than My Broken Parts
(6/10/19)

What a difference two years makes. Here I am, two years older and infinitely wiser. I must admit that the view on this side of the struggle is so much better. Have the last two years been easy?
Not. At. All.

In fact, it's probably been the hardest two years of my life, but also the most fruitful. As I surrendered my brokenness to God two years ago, He has, without me even realizing it, responded and restored me at the point of my brokenness. When you ask God to move and you're asking is according to His will, honey, He moves! Among myriad other things He's been working out in me over the last two years, as I looked back at those last three chapters, I realized that He also worked this brokenness out.

At the beginning of this year I recounted to my accountability partner that I was walking through the church one day and it hit me! As I was walking, it struck me that there was a new confidence that was now evident to me! I explained to her this invigorating sense I had as I moved with purpose through the church's middle level. I felt like I was walking with my head up and seeing the world, for the first time, face-to-face. I remember this moment like it was yesterday and I pray I always will. I recounted to her that, in that moment, it was clear to me that I had only seen the world from the ankle down… until that moment. Clearly I'm speaking figuratively, nonetheless, I'm speaking truthfully.

I wasn't even viewing that moment through the lens of the last three chapters. In truth, I hadn't revisited the writings of the last three chapters until now; and now, in light of them, that moment means so much more. I wondered why that sense came so clearly to me. It wasn't a special moment. I wasn't doing anything more than what I'm normally doing. I wasn't super dressed up and looking cute. I wasn't on my way up to the sanctuary for any special event. No, it was just a regular day and God met me there, in the midst of a regular day, with the answer to a two year old prayer.

You see, as I have continued to surrender my life to God over the last two years He has shown me so much more of who He's called me to be. He's shown me so much more of what He put on the inside of me. He's stripped away the lies that the enemy had caused me to believe. He's been teaching me my identity and as He's revealed identity, He's revealed purpose. As He's revealed purpose, He's revealed gifting. As He's revealed gifting, He's uncovered and renewed passion.

God has done exactly what I asked for two years ago and it is so much more significant than I ever knew. When I was willing to surrender that brokenness to Him, He was able to undo, in two years, what it took the enemy thirty-one years to do. The enemy had so layered me in masks and costumes — and so convincingly — that I had come to hate the woman I had become. I didn't like myself. Now it all makes sense; what I actually hated were the costumes the enemy had convinced me to put on over the years: victim, powerless, helpless, useless, ungifted, waste of space, purposeless, fruitless, and the list goes on. Then God showed me that none of that was who He created. That's why I couldn't tolerate what I saw in the mirror because, I wasn't looking at me. I was looking at the enemy's Frankenstein monster. Now I know who I am. I continue to learn what's inside me and God is showing me what I'm here for and I am blown away; but, this newfound (and still developing) confidence couldn't come until I surrendered my brokenness.

This new understanding of me, God's original design of me, couldn't come until I was willing to surrender the fact that I didn't know who I was. This new sense of purpose and passion couldn't come until I surrendered. I'm willing to bet that I'm not the only one who's come to the realization that, "I don't know me." The silver lining is once you've come to that realization, we know the one who does know the real you and I promise you; He is dying to introduce you to you... Or more accurately, He died already so that when you were ready you could come to Him yourself to learn the real you. The truth doesn't come without surrender; so, there's no activity after this chapter, because, there's nothing else to be said, only done. Let's get in our journals and start surrendering.

Sincerely,
In Pursuit of Surrender

"I was so over this singlehood just days ago, hours ago, moments ago... Thankfully, God has at least one more lesson to complete in my singlehood."

Surrendering The Need For Significance
(7/31/17)

Significance is the quality of being worthy of attention. I live in a constant dichotomous state. I long to be worthy of attention and, simultaneously, I long to not be the center of attention. How does that work, especially considering the gifting and calling God has placed in and on my life?

In public settings, I try to avoid the spotlight like a plague. In fact, when someone singles me out and all eyes fall on me, I get nervous and a little anxious, even. My breathing picks up, my heart starts racing, I start wringing my hands and I shrink with a bashful smile and averted eyes; yet, personally, I long to be in a relationship that affirms that I am worthy of attention. Not the attention of everyone, that's not my desire, just the attention of one. I believe that the major difference between those two sides of the attention coin is intimacy. I tend to be guarded amongst the masses but deep in my little introverted heart I desire intimacy — to know and be known.

Don't get me wrong, I have varying levels of intimacy with my family and amongst my friends, but

I find myself longing for a different kind of relationship now, a different kind of intimacy. I'm not talking about physical intimacy so put away your anointing oil; I'm still talking about the intimacy of knowing and being known. It's a pure desire, but, it becomes problematic when the desire for that intimacy and significance is what drives my actions. In previous seasons I had completely given in to satisfying that desire. I was willing to do just about anything to get and keep that intimacy.

The deeper issue was that the desire at that time was tainted by low self-esteem. I let that desire drive me to the wrong person and relationship. I compromised a lot to get what I thought I wanted and the truth is, once I had it, I was still miserable because I had traded so much to get it and it was so unstable. I felt like the rug could be pulled from under my feet at any moment. There was no guarantee, no commitment; and in my mind, because he wouldn't commit, it could all be gone in an instant. I had made it all about him and me, but the one it was never about was God. That was the real issue.

Today, I'm grateful that God has reminded me of that season and how far He's brought me. Today, I love myself more than I ever have before, but I'm also still learning to love myself as God does, unconditionally. Today, I'm grateful that this struggle with my desire for significance is just that, a struggle, because a couple of seasons ago it wasn't. I had given in and still didn't have what I needed which meant I was still miserable. Today, I'm grateful that God has changed my perspective and allowed me to see what He is yet teaching me in my singlehood. He's teaching me to agape myself so that I'll know agape when I see it in action—so that I'll see it when He sends it and not confuse it with any other form of love or lust or infatuation for that matter.

I was so over this singlehood just days ago, hours ago, moments ago. I felt like it had served its purpose and I had learned all I needed to learn from it—through it. I was tired of being alone and ready to move on to the next season. Thankfully, God has at least one more lesson to complete in my singlehood. For that I'm grateful; grateful that God won't allow my former insecurities (speaking life) to interfere with His destiny in my life.

"He needs me to understand my own design before He

launches me into destiny."

Before, I pursued love, relationship, acceptance and significance from a man because if he affirmed me, then I was off the hook. I didn't have to find myself worthy. But, that's not God's plan; He needs me to understand my own design before He launches me into destiny. I can't rely on someone else's opinion, affirmation or understanding of who I am.

Today, though I feel the pull of the need for significance, I have perspective. Today, I surrender it to God. I find my significance in Him. I find it in what His Word says about me. Today, I surrender my need to be found worthy of attention... to be found worthy, because He already says I am. His blood says I'm worthy. His scars say I'm worthy and more than 1,985 years before I was born He found me worthy of His attention on the cross. Then He settled the matter when He said, "It is finished." With those three words he said to me that self-doubt is finished. Self-hatred is finished. Low self-esteem is finished. Ignorance of self is finished. Caring way too much about human opinion is finished. And this desire to satisfy the need for significance by any means necessary is finished. Today, I find my worth in Him and this time I choose to believe Him. It. Is. Finished.

Sincerely,
In Pursuit of Surrender

Reflection Questions

Have you ever felt the pull of the need for significance in any area of your life?
Yes ☐ No ☐

If so, what are some things, in retrospect, that you did to try to satisfy this need for significance?

To see the full set of reflection questions, turn to page 92 in your IPoS Journal

"Ask and it will be given to you
Seek and you will find
Knock and the door will be opened to you
Just ask, just ask"
~Anthony Evans, Ask

Surrendering Timidity (A.K.A. Timid Faith)
(8/6/17)

On August 23rd, 2017, Pastor Travis Greene was smack dab in the middle of a life-altering ministry moment as a guest worship artist at our Fifth Pastoral Anniversary Community Night of Worship and he said something so powerful that it stuck even in this "slip n' slide" I call a memory. Most things come in my mind one side and slip right through to the other side before promptly sliding out of my memory; however, this moment is permanently embedded.

Pastor Travis said, "Fear is not an emotion, it's a spirit. The Bible says, 'God has not given us a spirit of fear[33].'" Then, he went on to say, "We try to give fear little cute names like timid and shy…"

Talk about a wake-up call! Those words resonated and stuck with me for the past two weeks since they were spoken. It's only just now, though, that God made it clear exactly why He caused those words to

---

[33] *2 Timothy 1:7*

prick my heart. Today, as I was reading my YouVersion Bible App devotional, God made it abundantly clear that He wanted me to seek Him about faith. As I did He led me to Mark 11:22-24, a familiar passage.

After Jesus curses a fig tree, He and His disciples pass by it the next morning and find it withered. The disciples are surprised and Jesus essentially says, "why are you surprised? Have faith in God." Then Jesus says these words, "Therefore I tell you, whatever you ask for in prayer, believe that you have received it and it will be yours."

Jesus spoke those words and as I read them something in me burned. I've heard them before, read them before, probably even spoke them out loud and still didn't fully believe them to be true for me. But, there is something about encountering a specific Word of God in the right season... There are powerful sermons, scriptures, sayings and even songs that, when spoken or presented to us at the wrong time, will fall flat. Months later, that same sermon, scripture, saying or song will come to mind and when you revisit it, you wonder how you could've been previously unmoved by it. You know how that's possible? *kairos*—God's appointed time. Yes, we are back on that conversation but only for the briefest moment, I promise. He knows exactly what we need and when we need it. He knew that today I needed to read that scripture again.

Guys, listen, when I read that scripture, I was so encouraged and filled with conviction all at the same time. Something in me clicked and immediately I thought of how timid I had been in my faith. "And without faith it is impossible to please God[34]..." That's not something that's just occurring to me; that's today's verse of the day! Talk about confirmation! I have been so utterly passive in my faith that it's not even funny. The more alarming truth is that I didn't even realize it. I had been so carefully lulled into this trap of passive faith that I was completely oblivious.

Well, today God made me aware of it, and today is exactly where it will stay; because today I choose to surrender timidity. You see, my timid, passive faith was rooted in fear.

"What if I take a bold stand and ask for the biggest, most intimidating desire of my heart and God says, 'No'?" Or "What if I ask God for the desire of my heart and make a bold declaration of faith and then God doesn't do it? I'd look like an idiot!" Or worse yet... the one of which I'm most guilty, "Well... I know God can, but... no, I won't ask."

I've convinced myself that those dreams and visions that my heart desires are selfish, though

---

[34] *Hebrews 11:6*

they're not. I've convinced myself that maybe they're not God's will, although He has overwhelmingly shown me that they are. I've talked myself out of just asking so many times and in so many ways that I've lost count. When I did ask, I immediately began backtracking and dialing my request back until it was almost unrecognizable. Why? Timid faith.

Today, it occurs to me that there are blessings that I've either missed or prolonged their coming because my faith wasn't audacious enough to ask or believe once I had asked. No more! I believe God! So today, I surrender timidity and instead I pick up courage and boldness like that of Hananiah, Mishael and Azariah. Boldness to say, "If I am thrown into the blazing fire, the God I serve is able..." and the courage to say, "... But if He does not[35]..." No more timidity! No more timid faith! God has unearthed the warrior in me, and I won't hide her again!

Sincerely,
In Pursuit of Surrender

---

[35] *Daniel 3*, the entire chapter gives the account of Hananiah, Mishael and Azariah; but verses 17 & 18 are specifically referenced here.

Just Ask
(6/19/19)

A few years ago, I received what was, at that time, the greatest birthday gift I'd ever received. My sister and my best friend pulled together and got me a VIP Ticket to attend the Kingdom Family Conference with Pastor, Dr. Tony Evans, Chrystal Evans Hurst and *drum roll*... Anthony Evans! They knew I'd been an Anthony Evans fan since about 2012 when his witness and testimony through music completely caught me off guard because it sounded like mine.

While at the conference, Anthony sang one of my favorite songs from his Real Life/Real Worship album, Ask. The song is taken straight out of Matthew 7:7-8. I love the song, but on this night, after Chrystal spoke an incredibly powerful word that found my heart like a heat-seeker missile, Anthony began to minister this song that I knew and loved. That night, the song meant something completely different. As he sang those words, "Ask and it will be given to you. Seek and you will find. Knock and the door will be opened to you. Just ask..." hot tears rolled down my face and although they didn't sting my cheeks, they stung my spirit. In that moment God was challenging me. He asked me the question,

"Why have you stopped asking?"

In that sanctuary, I had to fess up to God that I had stopped asking Him for things because I was afraid. I stopped asking because it seemed like every time I asked Him for something, He ignored me. I stopped asking because I no longer believed that He would do whatever I asked. I had stopped asking because I was afraid... and the weight of that truth that night left me standing in that sanctuary, undone, with tears pouring from my eyes.

In the four years since that night, God has been teaching me to be more bold in my faith. Specifically, in this last year or so, He's been teaching me about authority and the authority I have through the work of Jesus and His Holy Spirit. I will say that this is an area that I am yet surrendering, but I am definitely on the winning side of this battle. I continue to learn the depths of the authority I have access to because of the God to whom I'm connected. I am currently at the place where I am challenging myself to not just ask God to do something, but to exercise the authority He's given me to command this natural reality to get in alignment with the spiritual reality that He's already spoken over me.

In Joshua 10:12-13, there is an incredibly intriguing bit of truth recorded. In the heat of a battle against the Amorites, Joshua, the leader of the Israelites, declares to God and before his men, "Let the sun stand still over Gibeon, and the moon over the valley of Aijalon." Then, verse thirteen is where it gets really good! It reads, "So the sun stood still and the moon stayed in place until the nation of Israel had defeated its enemies." (NLT) Here was Joshua, in the middle of doing exactly what God told him to do and he was so zealous to do the work thoroughly that he wanted more daylight to complete the work.

More daylight. Have you ever been so overwhelmed with the work of the day that you just sat back and looked at it all and said to yourself, "There aren't enough hours in the day"? Then you let out a deep sigh and shook your head as you went back to what seemed like an impossible task. You know who never had that problem?! Joshua!!! Joshua saw the day getting later as he and his men were diligently destroying their foe and thought to himself,

"Ugh! If only it were daylight longer, we would jack these jokers ALL THE WAY up! Oh, I know... Lord, let the sun stand still right where it is so we can finish this work!"

Problem solved! Joshua needed more daylight to do his work, so he just asked in authority and boom, night stayed day and day stayed night!

Yet, when you observe the text closely, you come to understand that Joshua was actually commanding the sun to stand still, and he did so through his relationship with God. You see, Joshua knew that he was doing exactly what God had told him to do, and in order to do the work thoroughly he knew he needed a little more daylight; so, Joshua, with full confidence in God's authority to command day and night, tapped into his relationship with God and literally speaks to the sun. I kid you not, go look at the text! It says that Joshua prayed to God and literally spoke to the sun and told it to stand still. Then he spoke to the moon and commanded the same! Bruh! Sis! Do you see how epic this is?! Joshua knew his connection to God was in good standing, he knew that he was doing God's work and he had NO doubts about God's ability. Because of that, when Joshua's faith, met with an "impossibility" the "impossibility" had to move out of the way!

Holy Shrimp!!! Guys, that's the kind of boldness and courage I'm after! It was bold because... well, who commands the sun in full faith that the sun will obey; and it was courageous because he did it in front of others! He wasn't ashamed or afraid. There was not one doubt in Joshua's mind. He spoke and it happened, just like that.

It is accounts like this, in the scriptures, that won't allow me to settle for timid faith, a.k.a. fear! I am created in God's image and so are you. Just in case you forgot, the very first thing God did in Genesis chapter one was speak, "let there be light" and it was so! By the way, you do know that for those who have accepted Jesus Christ as their savior, the Holy Spirit of God lives on the inside of us, right?! You do know that when Jesus Christ died on the cross, he turned the tide, right?! All that I'm saying is that we have the authority to ask God for things and more than that to command those things, not for selfish personal-gain, but for the glory of God!

Guys, I don't know about you, but when I see accounts like this, it reminds me not to settle for what I see, but to speak, declare and command what God has spoken over me. To speak, declare and command those things that are not until they are[36].

" . . .when Joshua's *faith,* met with an

"*impossibility*" the "impossibility"

had to *move out of the way!* "

---

[36] *Romans 4:17b*

143

I have authority and so do you; however, we can't walk in the fullness of that authority until we surrender all of this fear that's been holding us back. My words have power, especially when they are in alignment with God's words. The issue is that fear puts a muzzle on me, so I don't speak, I don't declare and I don't command, which is the enemy's plan. But, enough is enough! I am made in the image of my Heavenly Father! I am His baby, and "nobody puts baby in a corner[37]!" (I couldn't resist) So, I'm still committed to my decision to surrender this fear, this timid faith, so that I can operate in the fullness of God's authority extended to me! So, the next time you see the sun stand still in the sky, just know that, that means, I've surrendered all of that fear and now... I'm unstoppable!

Sincerely,
In Pursuit of Surrender

---

[37] Dirty Dancing movie reference

Reflection Questions

What have you been afraid to ask God for?

Have you examined your request, your faith and your motives for asking? (See James 1:6-8 and James 4:2-3)
Yes ☐ No ☐

* To see the full set of reflection questions, turn to page 98 in your IPoS Journal

"Can't you just keep all these hormones and give them to me as a wedding gift?"

Surrendering My Biology
(Started: 10/5/17, Finished: …. 3 months later…)

Welp… I've successfully put off writing this entry for a month… and a half… Okay fine; almost two months! Happy now?! *mutters under breath* "Confess your sins one to another, He says[38]…" I digress. I put off writing this because… well, 'cuz I didn't wanna! *pouts and crosses arms*

Clearly I'm feeling animated today, but, I'm willing to bet that you've been here too; procrastinating because you don't feel like doing what you know you should. You should know though, that's another way of trying to exercise some power, a.k.a. control. Let's face it; we've all got a little Janet Jackson in us; if we didn't I wouldn't be writing this book. I knew I needed to write this entry because I knew I needed to submit my biology but I didn't feel like it so I procrastinated and therein lies the problem. I let my biology control my actions instead of being controlled by the Holy Spirit. I'm reminded of Ephesians 5:18, "Don't be drunk with wine… instead be filled with the Holy Spirit." (NLT) Y'all, I might

---

[38] *James 5:16*

not drink, but I was sho' nuff sippin' my own Kool-Aid! Well, I've had enough of that foolishness; so, here I am writing about submitting my biology… finally.

I can remember when I was younger and would hear people talk about this "biological clock" phenomenon. They talked about how a woman's biological clock can kind of cause panic or frenzy once she's reached a certain age. It was suggested during this biological clock conversation that women sometimes resort to desperation and settling in relationships; that there is this interesting shift that takes place when a woman reaches a certain age and the window within which she should or could have a child begins to get more narrow. Now, I don't remember how old I was when I first began learning about this biological clock phenomenon, but I do remember thinking something like, "I want no parts of that, whatsoever!"

Welp… Now I'm thirty-two (at the time of this writing), unmarried, single and doing my best to honor God in my body which means that I'm celibate and have been for seven and a half years and I will be until I'm married… Aaaaaaaaaaaaand, at this point in my life I've come to the conclusion that hormones suck! Utterly, thoroughly and completely suck! I think that these hormones should just be post-manufacture add-ons that come only with the

"Marriage Starter Pack." I think they should only be sold on late night infomercials for twelve easy payments of $1999.99. I think we should all just be ~~happily~~ stoically Vulcan until we say, "I do!"… Okay, so perhaps I'm exaggerating my annoyance just the slightest bit, but, my goodness! I understand what all the conversations were about now. Thankfully, now that I'm smack dab in the middle of womanhood, I have a better vantage point and context.

Now, if you are a guy and you're still reading this entry, you're probably going to want to tune out for a while, BUT don't do it. Guys don't check out on me because I'm willing to bet that there is at least one woman in your life that you love. That could be a mother, sister, daughter, cousin or perhaps you're believing God for a wife. Do yourself and every woman you love — past, present and future — a favor, KEEP READING! The next pages may make you a little uncomfortable but they'll make you a lot wiser and when it's all said and done, there's something here for you too. So, let's get to it!

I will start by saying that the most asinine part of my procrastination these past two months is that I was pretending that I'd never again encounter the circumstances that caused me to write that heading down two months ago. The truth is, God knew exactly what He was doing when He had me write that heading. He knew that almost precisely a month after writing the heading and abandoning the entry I'd be reminded why I needed to write this. He also knew that, should I remain disobedient that following month and put off writing again, I'd be reminded once more almost precisely one month after that, and so on and so forth, until I stopped being hard-headed. God is nothing if not patient.

For those of you reading this who still haven't figured out what I'm referring to, I'm talking about that very beautiful... special... magical time every month... when a woman's uterus falls out! (Side Note: I swear, if I could make this like a children's book, I'd put a little mirror on this page so that every guy who's reading could see his own face when he read that.) I digress. Guys, if you made it through that statement without puking or passing out, bravo; you should be just fine for the rest of this entry. For all of you who did puke or pass out... suck it up, Buttercup. I'm kidding. LOL......... *whispers* No, I'm not. But, no worries, if you were able to come back and keep reading then I'm confident you'll make it to the end.

All jokes aside though, God's design of the human body is no less than genius. But, His design of the female body is nothing short of miraculous. That being said, it's also frustrating as heck! Every month, when a woman comes to the end of her cycle (normally between 28-32 days) there is a 3-7 day period when she experiences... well, her period. Luckily for us women-folk, God doesn't restrict the fun to just one week, 'cuz, why just one week when it can be so many more! Did you taste that lovely sarcasm? If not, go back and read it again, but this time, sarcastically! (Go ahead. I'll wait...) Anyway, I digress. Every woman is different and as we all differ, so too do our cycles. That being said, I will speak specifically from my own experience, after all, it is my own biology I'm surrendering here. For my other ladies reading this, as I share my experience, I encourage you to think about your own monthly experience. Think about how it's similar and how it differs. If you've never done it before, ladies, I encourage you to think through and even begin to keep a log so you can see:

1) when your cycle starts and ends,
2) mood and thought pattern shifts surrounding your cycle each month
3) any spiritual struggles you encounter around that time each month.

Let me be further clear; you can notice these shifts during the week that your uterus falls out (LOL) or in the preceding or following weeks. I encourage you to do this, sisters, because whether you realize it or not, your emotions, hormones, thoughts and spirit are running in cycles too. After keeping this log for a few months, I'm willing to bet that you will notice trends. I did. I noticed that in the week preceding my period I became more emotional. By that I mean, by the grace of God I don't generally have mood swings, but I am more liable to cry or be emotionally heightened during this time. Now, that doesn't mean that I just burst into random tears, just that it takes less to get me to cry during this time (happy tears or sad tears). I also may get more easily irritated and have even less tolerance for foolishness than normal.

I know, these seem like trivial things or things that may only be important as it relates to my interpersonal relationships and the ways that I interact with my family and friends; however, it is important to note that these are all important things to know because the enemy tracks my cycle like a scent dog. He knows when I'm more emotionally susceptible and irritable and you'd better believe that he has a standing appointment on his calendar to find a way to try me every month. Chiiiiiild, he was tracking my cycles before I was and that gave him an advantage… a serious advantage over me.

Recently, though, I've noticed that in the week prior to my period I would become more…*leaves momentarily to look up a prettier synonym for horny (yes, gentlemen, women feel this way too)*… concupiscent. Isn't that a pretty word? But, y'all what happens in my mind, if I am not careful, during this time is decidedly UNPRETTY, okay!

This was important for me to realize because my thought life is one of the places I've struggled in for most of my thirty-two years. I've struggled with low self-esteem and negative self-talk, but I've also struggled just as much with lustful thoughts. There are reasons why these have been some of my most prevalent thought struggles but more about that in later chapters. The point is, I am already predisposed to lustful thoughts, so when this particular week rolls around every month and my hormones are shifting, I need to be prepared for an increased mental attack that heightens my natural sexual desires. I need to be mindful that the enemy is not impressed by my conviction to remain celibate until marriage. This means that he tries any and everything he can to get me outside of the will of God because if he can get me out of line in any area, he will exploit that area until he can get me out of alignment in every area.

> *"Imagine that, an acceptable sin!"*

That's his goal, to get a foothold. Now, let me just give you the trigger warning right now. This next part is about to get incredibly transparent and bumpy; buckle up.

For me, this attack has looked like this: since the enemy couldn't get me to have sex again before marriage, he decided to try to convince me that masturbation, pornography and explicit sexual fantasies were acceptable alternatives. Imagine that, an acceptable sin!

I'll tell you, that lucifer (little "l" 'cuz we put no "respeck" on his name) is a tricky one. It's just an iteration of the same trick he used in Eden! In Eden he asked, "Did God really say…" To me it was, "Did God really mean that you couldn't experience any sexual satisfaction before you were married? It's okay if it's not with another person, right?"

Then he took the deception a step further, "What does He expect you to do with these desires? He gave them to you."

Y'all, I'm not gonna lie, I partook. I ate the fruit! I ate the apple, the plum, the peach, the whatever fruit it was in the garden; that's what I ate! And what's worse, I didn't eat the fruit because I actually believed the enemy, I ate it because I wanted to believe him. I ate it because the thoughts sometimes got so thick in my mind that it felt like masturbation was the only way to get relief from the lustful thoughts and sexual desires in overdrive. So, I chose "the lesser" of the evils; but the lesser of two evils is still evil.

Let me tell you a secret… lean in… I've overcome this attack before without giving into the spirit of perversion which, I've since learned, is the spirit that was provoking me to masturbation, pornography and indulging in lustful fantasies. Ask me how?

"How, Ange?"

I'm so glad you asked! I overcame it by submitting it before it came. At my home church, our women's Bible study was working through a book study and the author challenged us to pray over our menstrual cycles. Why hadn't I thought about doing that before?! It seems like common sense. When your laptop starts giving you trouble, you consult the manufacturer, you consult the help desk. You consult someone who intimately knows the inner workings of your laptop. So, when I'm having an issue internally — be it physical, mental, emotional or spiritual — why not consult the one who fully and intimately knows my inner workings? Duh! I should've had a V8. Anyway, I decided to act on that challenge and IT WORKED! I didn't have any of the struggles that I normally would, all because I was intentional to set an appointment on my calendar to pray and surrender my cycle, my very biology, to God before the battle came. Then, I became lazy with my surrender and before I knew it I had slipped right back into old patterns because I wasn't intentional about my surrender.

So, why did I spend so much time talking about a woman's cycle? The fact that a woman's physical body operates in cycles helps to illuminate the fact that, if we're diligent to observe carefully, so, too will we see that our spiritual, mental and emotional journeys can travel in cycles. Have you ever gone through a test and then a while later had déjà vu? You wonder to yourself and sometimes to God why you have to keep going through the same thing over and over. The answer is that the enemy knows your buttons and will press them every chance he gets, in an effort to cause you to fall and God will allow it for three reasons:

- to remind us of just how much we need Him,
- to give us opportunities to grow, and
- to give us an opportunity to see just how much He has grown us.

Cycles—ladies and gentlemen, we all have cycles (insert pitch perfect Jonathan McReynolds run). Now that we've come full circle in this discussion, let's get to the real nitty gritty. Y'all, we were not created to be mastered by our cycles, but to master them. We were not made to be mastered by our physical bodies; we were made to master them. In the last verse of 1 Corinthians 9, the Apostle Paul encourages us to make our bodies submit so that we can run this race well, to win the prize at the end.

We are a spirit that possesses a soul and inhabits a physical body. These bodies that you and I live in are not who we are, they only house who we are. Our bodies put us through some changes! Hormones are released in the brain and work their way through our bodies and trigger desires and thoughts and behaviors. But, there is something else that inhabits this body too.

When you and I accept Christ as our Savior, God's Holy Spirit comes to dwell with us, in us.[39] In case you're not keeping score that's spirit-2, flesh-1. On our own, we are helpless to make our flesh, our bodies, and our hormones submit to Christ; but when we rely on the Holy Spirit, our biology doesn't stand a chance. God is the one who created these bodies to house our spirits, so He is the one who can call them into order and command them to obey. Through the Holy Spirit, we have authority!

"Don't become lazy

in your surrender."

---

[39] If, by chance, you're reading this and have never prayed the prayer of salvation to invite Jesus into your heart and you'd like to, please see Index A at the back of the book. It's a decision you won't regret.

Today… finally, exactly 3 months after I started, I am ready to actually surrender my biology. That being said, there are two pieces of encouragement I want to offer to you before we surrender this time. First, I am transparent about how long it took me to get to the place of actual surrender because, IT'S RIDICULOUS and funny and REAL… but, mostly, ridiculous. Second, I'm so transparent because I want you to see… no, God wants you to see what process looks like. As you walk through this journey of surrender, some things will be easier to surrender than others; please know that easy or hard, long or short, it is all a process. Don't be discouraged if you are surrendering something to God and you don't see the change you want to see as soon as you want to see it. I promise you that from the moment you pray the prayer to surrender it to God, He is working on your behalf. Just hang in there through the process.

I want to offer this admonishment - remember when I said I had overcome this biology thing before? I wasn't lying. I actually did overcome it, but there are some things that need to be constantly surrendered to God. As long as we live in these bodies we will constantly need to surrender something about them to God. Don't stop surrendering it! Don't become lazy in your surrender and slip back into old habits. Now I think I thoroughly ~~understand~~ overstand that "thorn in the flesh" thing that Paul talked about[40].

Maybe there is something in your body other than the typical, clinical hormonal changes that you need to surrender. Maybe you have chronic pain, or some other illness — temporary or chronic. Whatever challenges this body is presenting you with, I know the one who masters every challenge and He cares for you. So, today, join me in prayer as we surrender this biology to the one who created it and can master it all.

Sincerely,
In Pursuit of Surrender

Prayer of Surrender: My Biology

Faithful Father,

You are The Master Craftsman. Only You could create the human body out of the infinite creativity of Your mind. You have masterfully knit us together and given every part of our body a purpose beyond our understanding. I thank You for how You've created me. I thank You for the way You've created my body to work. But, if I'm honest, sometimes I

---

[40] *2 Corinthians 12:7-10*

struggle with this body. I know that everything we go through has a purpose. So, I thank You that in dealing with my biology, both the natural functioning of it, and the malfunction of it, You are teaching me to master this flesh.

Remind me that I live in this flesh, but this flesh is not who I am. Remind me that my spirit has the ability, responsibility and authority to command my flesh and so today I command my flesh to be surrendered to You. I recognize that You've created my body to work in cycles and up until now, this cycle has mastered me. But, I thank You for the knowledge that I don't have to be subject to my cycle, in fact, when I exercise the authority given through Jesus Christ, my cycle is subject to me.

Daddy, I lay this body and all of its inner-workings at Your feet. I declare, in faith, that my thoughts and actions will no longer be guided by the hormones my body releases, instead I will be controlled by The Holy Spirit. I choose, today, to be surrendered to You completely; and that means mastering this flesh by surrendering it to You.

Dad, would You step in and do what I can't? Teach me to beat my flesh into submission so that I will not be dragged into sinful thought and behavior patterns when natural desires occur. Please remind me that desires to be physically intimate with the opposite sex are normal and even God-given; but also remind me that I was not made to act on those desires before the appointed time. In fact, in the Song of Solomon, you implore me to not awaken love before its time. So, teach me to surrender those natural desires to You when they occur (and before they get out of hand), and not to beat myself up for them.

I thank You for the fact that You are Lord even over this body that I live in, and it must come under authority. Dad, I give You all of me and I ask You to give me victory over this flesh by teaching me to master it instead of being mastered by it. I thank You that all of these things are already done in the mighty and the matchless name of Jesus, Amen.

Sincerely,
In Pursuit of Surrender

"I'll write a clever quote here.............. tomorrow."
~Guess Who.....

Surrendering Procrastination
(1/16/18)

In the last chapter we talked about a constant companion of mine. This dude and I go way back. We go back like Adidas track suits and gold chains; and even though I don't even like this dude like that, I defend him every time somebody tries to put him on blast. I'm willing to bet you do too. Does this sound familiar:

"I just work better under pressure."

Or what about this, if you're reading this book with a Bible study group, you didn't start reading this chapter until right before your group study time started and you just skimmed enough to know what to say to sound like you spent some time in His presence about it. Heck, me too and I wrote the book! …Yeah, so you're cool with this dude too, huh? No worries. God is going to help us surrender this monkey on our backs.

Now, if I didn't know and have relationship with Jesus I'd say we are hopelessly at the whim of this procrastination beast. However, since I do know Jesus and have relationship with Him, I can say one thing for certain, two things for sure:

1) we are not hopeless, nor helpless because we serve the God who has all power and all authority over all things all the time, and

2) procrastination is not a beast; it's a spirit and not the one you think.

When we were adolescents and our parents asked us to do something — normally, that we didn't want to do — we would say, "okay" and keep right on doing whatever we were doing because we had silently decided we'd do it in our own time. But, why? We knew it would inevitably result in us getting the taste slapped out of our mouths or us awakening, bewildered, wondering how we time travelled into the middle of next week or, more likely, BOTH! We knew exactly what the consequences of our actions were yet we did it anyway! Why?! Are we all masochists?! Well, that's a debate for another day. Almost certainly the reason why we did it every time is that we didn't want to be told what to do. We especially didn't want to be told to do what we didn't want to do in the first place. Nevertheless, we knew that if our parents said it, we eventually had to do it. Simply explained, because we resented being told what to do, we wanted to exercise some semblance of control over our own lives. We figured that if we had to do it, we would decide when it got done.

I told you earlier, procrastination is not a beast, it's not just a noun, as a dictionary would suggest, it's a spirit that breeds sin. I was having a conversation about procrastination with a dear sister-friend of mine and as we spoke the Lord made it very clear to me what procrastination really was and the danger that lurks when it goes unchecked. In James 1:15 the writer says, "Then, after desire has conceived, it gives birth to sin, and sin, when it is full grown, gives birth to death."

That means that sin never starts as it ends. It may start off as a cute little toddler mouthing off to their parents as they throw a massive tantrum, but it may end in a tearful courtroom where that full-grown toddler threw a full-grown tantrum and took someone's life. Now, I am by no means saying that a cute little mouthy toddler will end up in prison, I'm not saying that at all. I'm simply using that visual to demonstrate how sin works.

I mean, who doesn't love laughing at sassy toddlers on YouTube or Facebook? They're cute as little miniatures, sassing on and on about not wanting to go to bed. It's their cute little hands and their cute little voices and their cute little hand gestures and their cute little everything! However, unchecked, they may become not so little teenagers with foul mouths and an unhealthy disdain for authority.

Every sin starts somewhere. Catch it in its infancy and make it subject to Jesus Christ because what God revealed to me, as clear as day, as I spoke with my friend is that the root of procrastination is rebellion—Period. Rebellion may not be your intention, but the enemy only cares about your intentions inasmuch as he can pervert and distort them.

When we procrastinate, we intend to return and complete a task at a time that is more convenient for us. We intend to complete the task, just not right now. Now, consider this, God's timing is perfect. God's timing doesn't operate like ours, remember? He operates in *kairos*. We've talked about this Greek word for time that literally means "the appointed time" or "the proper time." Just as a refresher, the way that we understand time is *chronos*, a space of time or measurable time. *chronos* is the root of our English word, "chronological." We understand time as a measurable passing or dispensation of time. We count time by the seconds, minutes, hours, days, weeks, months, years and so on. We have a million and one ways to reference time: decades, centuries, millennia, but I dare say there is no one alive who can say they've personally lived through and experienced centuries with an 's.' But not only has God experienced all of the centuries in the history of the world, He's orchestrated them. Because He is the creator and orchestrator of all time, He is not bound by it as we are.

I know, I know, you're thinking that we've already had this talk about time, but it is imperative for me to revisit this conversation to make it clear just how important this concept is in general and specifically as it relates to surrendering procrastination. It is important for us to understand God's perspective of time in order to make this next part clear. Since we operate in *chronos*, when we procrastinate we have decided to put off for a later dispensation of time what is more aptly handled in the present. However, because when God is asking us to do something at a specific time He has the understanding of what is the appropriate time (*kairos*) for that task, He asks us to do it right on time. When we choose to procrastinate, we run the risk of missing His k*airos*, the opportune moment. If we don't do what God has asked us to do at the moment He's asked us to, we've missed the window and that is disobedience. Doing the right thing at the wrong time is still wrong.

Let's revisit the battlefield analogy. Imagine you are there in a fox hole and the enemy is firing relentlessly trying to take you out. Over the radio you hear, "fire at will" but you freeze there because you think that it's best to wait until the enemy fire slows down and you'll just fire once you know it's safer. Maybe you freeze because you just don't feel like coming out of your fox hole at that moment. Then you hear, "Cease fire! Repeat, cease fire!" crackle over the radio. You then hear the enemy fire slowing down across the battlefield and you decide "That's my cue. This is my moment." You spring up and spray machine gun fire across the battlefield before you realize the opposition was walking across unarmed with a white flag waving. You were given a specific order at a specific time from someone with a better vantage point of the battlefield, but you missed the window within which you were to obey that order and you made a fatal mistake. If we make a habit of continually missing that window, then we have made rebellion our habit.

Indeed, procrastination is not just a noun, it is also a spirit and we don't have to be subject to spirits unless we choose to be. We don't have to obey spirits but because of the Holy Spirit dwelling in us and by His authority, those spirits must obey us.

So today, make a different choice. Don't continue to choose obedience to a deadly spirit because you like its costume. Make no mistake, the root of procrastination is rebellion. Therefore, I make a decision today and every day to stop being willfully disobedient to God by putting off for later what He requires of me now. This is one of those things that you and I are going to have to continually and aggressively surrender to God. This will be a hard one to surrender but I still choose to do it. Why? Because God is asking me to do it, and He's asking me to do it right now. No more rebellion.

Will you let it go today? Will you release the sin of rebellion? You can do everything through Jesus Christ because He gives you strength to do it[41]. Stop putting off for tomorrow what is required of you today because the day will come when we all have to give an account for every word, every deed and every misdeed and that's the one task that none of us can put off for later. Surrender it today and every day. Surrender it now.

Sincerely,
In Pursuit of Surrender

Follow-Through
(6/19/19)

When you have been in the habit of procrastinating, it can be hard to do something different because a stronghold has taken up residence in your mind. Take the opportunity to speak with

---

[41] *Philippians 4:13*

God and your accountability partner/group about ways to remain accountable in this journey of surrendering procrastination. Also, pray with them, in authority, to break the stronghold that procrastination has built in your mind and in your life. Remember, you are not at the mercy of the spirit behind procrastination, which is rebellion. It is actually subject to you when you speak with the authority of Jesus Christ.

Finally, don't pray just once, pray continually; again, we are not dealing with an ordinary sin, we are dealing with a spirit that has created a stronghold that has formed a way of life. It will take consistency and intentionality to break it. Don't give up!

Sincerely,
In Pursuit of Surrender

"I don't feel like feeling like giving up what I'm feeling, like adoption; But today it's not an option."

~Me

Surrendering My Emotions
(2/3/18)

Confession Time: Soooooooo.............. there was this guy. Once upon a time, I had been crushing on him mostly from afar. Then, I actually met him and had gotten to know him and his character a little better. Needless to say, if I used all of the heart eyes emojis in all the world it wouldn't be enough to express the magnitude of my, then current, swoon level for this brotha. Yes, people who love Jesus can swoon too. No, it doesn't secretly reveal that we don't love Jesus enough. And no, I won't debate these facts with you. LOL.

Anyway, I digress. So, a while ago, I was thinking about this brotha and the magnitude of the swoon in my spirit (LOL) and my feelings for him just really hit me hard. So, in the middle of my workday, in the middle of thinking of him, I just started praying, nothing deep; and it wasn't even a new concept. I had prayed for him before. God had even challenged me to pray for him for a period of time. I took it as God's way of saying,

"Well, if you gon' be thinking about the brotha all the time, then you might as well pray for him when you think of him."

So, I'd prayed for him before. I'd also prayed for clarity and direction from God concerning him. I'd done all that before, but there was something different about this prayer. This was a prayer of surrender.

When the weight of my feelings for him hit me, I knew that what I needed was to not act on my feelings in that moment; to not make up a reason to text him. What I needed was to do something that I haven't done in years and relationships past. I needed to surrender my emotions. I've tried what "the culture" says. I've done what felt good in the moment. I've lived according to my feelings before and they led me down a road that seemed sunny and bright at first but very quickly turned dark and treacherous. I was swiftly headed to spiritual death and were it not for divinely placed accountability in my life at that time, I would have surely fallen off of the cliff on which I was teetering. Needless to say, I have been there and done that, I'm not doing it again.

I know some of you are probably reading this and thinking, "It is not that serious, Ange." But, I promise you, it is. One of the things I admire about young King David (before he ever assumed his role as king, officially) was that he sought God even in seemingly small things. He sought God in situations that seemed like they were no-brainers. He sought God in the middle of great distress. This dude was seeking God no matter what!

One such instance that comes to mind is the account found in 1 Samuel 30. David and his fighting men had gone off to fight but were sent back home. When they arrived at home, they found that their camp had been raided and burned and all of their families had been taken captive. David and his men—his big, strong, ferocious fighting men—cried out and mourned their families there in the midst of those ruins. (Side Note: Real men know that it's okay to cry. Just saying... I digress) They were hurting and rightfully so, but, very quickly their hurt turned to anger and their anger became misplaced; they were considering killing David.

In the midst of all of this, David sought God. Now, David was a warrior surrounded by other warriors; you would think that after they had their cry and got good and angry that they'd go pursue the ones who were responsible. However, before acting in emotion, before doing what he felt, David sought God. He asked God if he and his men should pursue the Amalekites. What?! If the Amalekites take my family AND I'm a warrior... (excuse my country talk for just a moment) I'm finna go and take the fight to them and there's gon' be some furniture moving all up and down that countryside; ya hearrrd me?! But, no. In the midst of his grief, in the midst of uncertainty about whether his men would kill him or not, David sought God. David's emotions take a back seat to God's presence and His Word.

That's where I find myself today. My emotions are strong, compelling even, but they're not smart. Dr. Tony Evans says, and I agree that, our emotions don't have intellect. I like to say, our emotions are strong as all outdoors, but they are dumb as a pile of bricks. My emotions don't know and don't care about the truth that I was not meant to be led by them. It is up to my spirit to command my soul.

Today, I choose to make my emotions obedient to God. These lovely butterflies I feel are wonderful, but they don't get to tell me what to do anymore. I choose to surrender these emotions to God and let Him be the one to inform them. What emotions are you wrestling with? Will you make this choice with me today? Don't wait until you feel like it because you may never feel like it. But when you know better, you do better, whether you feel like it or not.

Sincerely,
In Pursuit of Surrender

The Best of My Love
(6/19/19)

I'll tell you, this chapter, specifically, has revolutionized my approach to attraction, dating and relationship. Before, emotion was one of the most important factors of the "attraction dance." I mean, think about it, "I'm feeling him, but is he feeling me?" So, we'd put out feelers, drop hints or just outright ask the brother. Sometimes, by the time the brother gets back to you with an answer, you realize that it was just a momentary infatuation, and you're not as interested as you initially thought.

Feelings. They can get you into a world of trouble. It's been a couple of years, and let me tell you how many times I've reminded myself or others that my/their feelings don't get to be in control. That goes for any emotions—attraction emotions, sure; but also, anger, worry, fear, you name it! We're allowed to feel them; in fact, we're supposed to, but then submit them to God and let Him be the one to inform the emotions. Our emotions are just as fickle as people. Think about it, we're happy one moment and mad the next; and we're seriously considering keeping our emotions in charge?! It's a 'no' for me. There was actually one particular instance at the end of last year, leading into this year, when I got to put this surrender to the test.

There was another guy whom I actually know much better than the dude from a few years ago. I know this man to be truly godly, funny, kind, admirable and did I mention handsome?! He's a really great guy and we've been friends for a couple of years now. When I first met him, immediately my flesh went into overdrive, "He loves God AND he looks like that?!?! Holy Father!!!!!!"

Nonetheless, I quickly sought God and asked Him to teach me to view this man as my brother in Christ first, because that would ensure that I view this man correctly and guard his heart accordingly. Initially, my flesh wanted to view him as a prospect—as potential— but my spirit knew he's my brother, first. When I view him as my brother first, my goal is to guard his heart well, and not to seduce his heart or entice him. So I prayed that prayer a couple of years ago, shortly after we met and God did that thing! Then, as I continued to get to know him more and speak with him more and observe him more... I fell in love with him. I know, my eyes are as big as yours right now! I can't even believe I'm writing about this, but this is what surrendering your emotions in real time looks like, so I've gotta share how God showed up in my surrender.

There I was at the end of 2018, just minding my business when "in love" came and slapped me like I stole something! Chiiiiiiiiiiild, I did what any self-respecting woman who loves God would do... I called my accountability partner! I may have been emotional, but I was not stupid! I called her to explain what was going on. I explained that, of course, I loved this man—he's my brother and my friend. Then I explained that, out of nowhere the love transformed and then "in love" rolled up into the party like it was invited. My exact words to her were,

"Soooooooooooo...... I love a man..." and we both instantly cackled into our cell phones.

She then promptly informed me that, that sounded like a country song. From that point on, my brotha's code name was developed. We called him "The Country Song." So, I trust you will indulge me for the remainder of this chapter as I refer to my friend as The Country Song (TCS). That's his name, for all of you Nosey Nancys and Nathans, The Country Song! I digress; I explained everything and referred to this chapter that I had written about not even a whole year prior. I told her that my plan was to surrender my emotions to God and to allow Him to inform them and I enlisted her prayers in the process.

So, I surrendered my emotions to God and I asked Him if my emotions were legitimate or if I'd allowed the enemy to get in and pervert God's initial intent for the love between The Country Song and me. Was I loving TCS rightly or had the phileo (friendship/brotherly love) that God intended been perverted by the enemy to try to cause me to get out of alignment? I asked God; but I intentionally didn't speak a word to TCS about it at that time. I prayed all through the end of last year and the beginning of this year until I believed I heard God give me clarity, but wasn't sure, so I just awaited His confirmation.

I believe confirmation came. I know that my friend, my brother, TCS, is meant to be just that, my friend and brother; and I am so satisfied with that answer. What's more, I'm grateful that God reminded me to surrender these emotions to Him before following my feelings and going to TCS first and perhaps creating an awkward situation. That would've really sucked because I love him as my brother and I'd never want to jeopardize that because I refused to check my emotions.

That, my friends, is just one instance of what surrendering our emotions looks like. There are myriad other ways that God desires to see us surrender our emotions: our hurt, our anger, our grief, our joy, our love, our everything. God can handle every emotion that we could possibly experience and He desires to, but we have to first be willing to surrender it. It doesn't matter how you feel so much as it matters what you do with how you feel.

Sincerely,
In Pursuit of Surrender

"Put faces on those moments you spend comparing yourself to others!"

Surrendering Comparison, Pt. 1
(10/24/18)

I am the third of four children. I have a little sister and two older brothers. I grew up a straight-up tomboy because I looked up to my brothers and wanted to be just like them. In retrospect, I realize how annoying I must've been to them because I was peeved to no end when our baby sister, Charysse — who is four years my junior — constantly followed me around copying everything I did and said. As she shadowed my every move, inevitably, I'd finally snap and beg my mom to make her stop. Each time, without hesitation, this lil' girl would retort,

"But, you're my role model!"

Over and over and over again, this was the pattern. Y'all, I promise, I wanted to rip my ears off and just throw 'em away! I hated hearing that phrase!

Well, my older brothers, Joseph and John, are seven and four years older than me, respectively. As you can imagine, there were countless opportunities for me growing up to whine to my mother,

"How come he gets to go and not me?! How come he can and I can't?!"

Quite frankly, that's to be expected. It's childish behavior, therefore, it's acceptable from a child's mouth; however... do you know what's not acceptable? Those words constantly ruminating in the mind of a full-grown woman. That's not okay! Why; because when I allow those thoughts to live in my mind or on my lips, I am telling God, over and over again, that He made a mistake. Now, since there are a couple different types of comparison that we will address here, we're gonna break this into two chapters. The first deals with comparing our person, abilities and gifting with that of others. Let's dig in right there.

Back in 2011 I had the privilege of being in a hilarious gospel comedy play called, "The Bold & The Sanctified," written and directed by a great friend, Sherri Lynn Johnson. I had a dual role in that I was mainly acting, but I also had a song in the show. Now, this wasn't like I was singing a solo verse and then the rest of the cast joined in and we took it on home. No, this was just me... onstage... with one other actor who was playing my best friend. All the vocals for this song were on me, with not even so much as a "shoo-doop" of background vocals. Now, if you read my bio at the back of this book, then you're probably wondering what the problem was. You're probably thinking, "Oh, okay. Well, she's a worship leader; that sounds about right." That's probably what Sherri Lynn thought when she offered me the role. Heck, truth be told, that's probably what everyone was thinking—"We already know she's an actor; AND she's a worship leader?! Perfect!" That is, everyone except me was probably thinking that. Guys, I. Was. TERRIFIED!!!

Let me paint the picture. Don't we always wanna paint the picture when we're trying to get someone to co-sign some foolishness?! (Lol) I digress; back to painting the picture. This show was a literal masterclass of Pittsburgh's finest gospel vocalists, and honey, let me tell you, Pittsburgh's got talent! So, here I am, I had only been leading worship for about two years at this point. I was just getting my sea legs. Add to that, I also had no idea of my identity. I had no clue what God had called me to. I had no clue what He placed in me. All I knew was that I loved singing and apparently I was "okay" enough to be asked and groomed to lead worship sometimes. Did I mention I had suffered with low self-esteem my entire life at that point?

Chiiiiiiild, I was doing just fine at rehearsals until it was time to start adding the music into our rehearsal time. Thankfully, at our first musical rehearsal, a great sister-friend of mine saw me and pulled me to the side to ask me what was wrong. I finally gave voice to the poison I had been chewing on. "Sherri's got all these amazing singers in the show; what does she need me for?"

Ugly, aren't they, the words we say to ourselves when we think no one is listening. That wasn't the first time I had said similar words to myself and unfortunately, it wouldn't be the last either. I've spent the vast majority of my life telling myself that other people are better at this, more qualified for that, prettier, thinner, *Shirley Caesar voice* YOU NAME IT! Nevertheless, while I was saying that to myself, what I was saying to God was,

"You should have made me look like her or sound like them. You put me together wrong. You were supposed to make me the skinny, pretty, outgoing girl with the voice of an angel and range like Mariah Carey!" (Hey, Mariah! We're friends... in my head. Me and Mariah go back like babies and pacifiers... I digress.) I was saying, "This is not right, God. I'm not right. Fix me."

That's what we've said to God when we've compared ourselves to others. I know it's hard, but read those words again, go ahead, I'll wait for you right here... How do those words make you feel? Now, imagine how they make our Father feel.

Before He placed us in our mothers' wombs, He took time to dream us up in His mind. His eyes lit up and His mouth curled into a smile as He spoke to Himself about what you'd be like. How hair number

85,213 would dance to the beat of its own drum and always curl opposite of the other 99,999 hairs on your head. How He would give you a passion to help people in a world full of selfish ambition. How He'd make you an introvert so that when you stood on stages around the world and people saw how boldly and unashamedly you shared the gospel; they would know that there is a God who can do anything. He perfectly engineered your smile so that it would pull to the right just a little. He painstakingly designed you, crafted you, gifted and equipped you and then He stepped back with a smile the size of infinity on His face and said, "She is very good. He is very good." Then, we, the created, turn to The Creator and say, "Oh, but you made a mistake. If you could just redo me and make me like person number 13,295,382 that would make me so happy. Thanks!" Heartbreaking. But, this is what we do to God every time we compare ourselves to others.

Let me be abundantly clear, God made absolutely zero mistakes when He created you; and in case you need to hear this, you were not an accident. God created you and sent you into time at exactly the right moment, fully equipped to respond to a need in the earth. Do you hear me? You were strategically created and placed in time to respond to a need in the earth. God built into you exactly what you need in order to accomplish that for which He purposed you. Yes, that's right, you have a purpose and it wasn't some ill-thought-out, clumsy, last-minute purpose. No, God spent time and energy crafting your purpose and crafting you for it.

Consider this, when you and I spend precious time whining to God that He made a mistake, we are wasting time that we could be using to walk in purpose. Or think of it this way, every moment we spend trying to be like someone else is a moment that the need we were created to meet goes unmet.

Those children that you are called to speak life into may only be hearing and believing words of death. That business that you are supposed to start that would create gainful employment in a disenfranchised community that's desperately in need of economic stimulus, while you're busy comparing, that community remains desolate. The lives of those innocent people that you are supposed to defend in a courtroom against a system built for their oppression are being destroyed. Put faces on those moments you spend comparing yourself to others. You see, every moment we waste comparing what we can do to what someone else can do is a moment of someone else's life that we're sacrificing on the altar of comparison.

The stage is set. The world is waiting for the sons and daughters of God to be revealed[42]; but, we can't be revealed because we're backstage complaining to

---

[42] *Romans 8:19*

our Director that Sister Suzie's or Brother Brandon's role should actually be ours. Hey, listen, lives are depending on us getting over ourselves! I'll share a secret with you that will hopefully help you get out of God's way in your life.

I mentioned that back in 2011 I had no idea who God had created me to be. I had no sense of identity, no sense of what the heck I was here for. Truth? The enemy was on a violent crusade to try and convince me that I was a marginally talented loser. Now, fast forward to 2018 (at the time of this writing). Now, more than ever, I have a better understanding of how and why God created me the way He did. I have a better understanding of what He put on the inside of me and of whom He's purposed me to serve. My vision is by no means 20/20 yet, but He's been fine-tuning my vision, understanding, wisdom, and gifting; and I'll tell you what, if I had known back then who He would've freed me to be in 2018, I would've spent my time trying to be like 2018 me instead of everyone else. And, 2018 me is just the tip of the iceberg!

I've said all of that to say this, when I became more intentional about silencing the voice of comparison and focusing in on what God was saying about my identity and calling, I was blown away by who He revealed me to be and what He called me to do. And let me reiterate that He's only shown me a portion. My mind is blown by just a portion of an understanding of my identity and calling; can you imagine understanding the fullness?!

The fact is, I never could have become 2018 Ange if I hadn't silenced the voice of comparison. That doesn't mean that comparison doesn't still come calling. It just means, thanks to the movie *Black Panther*, I now know what to do when comparison comes calling... *insert M'Baku bark* "You are not permitted to speak here!"

> *"You are so dope!"*

Colonizers, like comparison, are no longer permitted in my mind! Auntie Maxine Waters reclaimed her time and I'm reclaiming my mind!

That's the secret. When you silence the voice of comparison long enough for God to show you who you really are, what's inside you and what you're called to do, He will blow your mind so much that you won't waste your time trying to be like other people. You'll spend your time becoming who He called you to be! You are so dope! You just can't see it because you're wasting all your time looking at someone else. Stop it!

Today, let's focus on this kind of comparison, that comes from a lack of understanding of our true identity. Let me offer that the key is to start learning the truth of your identity and calling! Today, we are going to surrender our ignorance in favor of God's wisdom and revelation. We're gonna make the choice to stop focusing on everyone else and instead focus on what God says about us. Let's take a few minutes to go to God in prayer.

Sincerely,
In Pursuit of Surrender

"She's got more than me! That's not fair!"
~Every kid, ever

Surrendering Comparison, Pt. 2
"The Envy Monster"
(11/23/18)

In the last chapter, we discussed one form of comparison and alluded to another. We discussed comparing who we are to other people. Now we're going to deal with the comparison of what we have to others. To be transparent, I have absolutely been guilty of both kinds of comparison. I'm not proud of it, but the truth shall make you free[43]. Now, whereas the comparison in part one was rooted in ignorance (or rejection) of who we are, the type of comparison we're dealing with today is rooted in envy.

Just to be sure we're all on the same page, envy is not a feeling, it is a sin; and just so you know I'm not making it up, Exodus 20:17 says, "Do not covet your neighbor's house. Do not covet your neighbor's wife, his male or female slave, his ox or donkey or anything that belongs to your neighbor." To covet is to envy.

A quick note of clarification, jealously and envy, while similar, are not the same. God, Himself, tells us

---

[43] *John 8:32*

that He is a jealous God[44]. So clearly, because God's very nature is holy, jealously in its purest sense is not a sin. You see, jealousy refers to a longing for and fierce guarding of what is rightfully yours, especially when found in the possession of someone else; whereas, envy is longing for something that belongs to someone else.

For instance, if a will is read and Johnny has been legally left his parents' home, but Bonnie, his little sister, is living in the home and refuses to leave, well, then Johnny is jealous to claim what is rightfully his. But, let's say that Bonnie refuses to leave because she thinks the house should have been left to her instead. Well, Bonnie is envious of what Johnny has and has decided to act on the sin of envy by trying to take possession of what does not belong to her. Understand that Bonnie did not start operating in sin when she refused to relinquish possession of what did not belong to her; she operated in sin the moment she determined in her mind to want what very clearly did not belong to her.

Now, aside from the fact that we need to pray for Bonnie and Johnny, bless their little hypothetical hearts, hopefully, what you've gleaned from this made up family conflict is understanding. With this type of comparison, what we're really dealing with is the deeper seeded sin of envy. In the spirit of honesty,

---

[44] *Exodus 34:14*

transparency and healing, I'm going to share a very non-hypothetical story with you.

Approximately ten years ago (at the time of this writing), God led a very special woman to include me in a discipleship group that He had laid on her heart to facilitate. Let's call this special woman, Mama Bird. Mama Bird was obedient to take this group of ladies under her wing and pour into us and hold us accountable in even the most intimate and difficult areas of our lives. God specifically sent Mama Bird to me at a pivotal point in my life and He used her as a beacon of grace, love and gentle restoration. I am ever so grateful to God for sending Mama Bird to love, correct and nurture me. Because of her obedience, I was able to hear the truth of God's Word that was calling me to release a spiritually detrimental relationship, which, in turn, freed me to take this journey of purpose that I've been on with God for the last 8+ years. Needless to say, I will always love and appreciate my Mama Bird more than she could ever know, just for her obedience to God in that season of my life and beyond.

Now, when Mama Bird first began the discipleship group, she was a newlywed. Fast forward to about 2-3 years ago and Mama Bird has been married for several years now and has a couple of children. All of a sudden, whenever she stood to minister, there was a blockage in me. I could hear the words she was saying, and I could acknowledge they were true and full of power, but there was an internal battle for me to accept and apply God's Word coming through her. Weird, right? This woman, whom I love and admire, was doing what she was called to do, ministering in the wisdom and power of God and all of a sudden, I found it hard to receive from her.

For the last 2-3 years, that has been a struggle for me. Now, here's the really ridiculous part, I introspected and understood why it was difficult for me to receive from her, but I refused to put the proper name to it because as long as I didn't put "the name" on it, then I could continue to rationalize why I was justified in my feelings. So, for the last 2-3 years, I've refused to name it and continued to wrestle within myself. But 2018 is the year where the last of the old me came to die. About a month or two ago, I finally got tired of fighting this same battle, and I admitted to my accountability partner that I have been dealing with the sin of envy and it was particularly hurtful because the target of my envy was a woman that I love dearly. Whew, child! The weight lifted when I finally put the proper name to it and confessed my sin! Now, I could face it and deal with it!

Now, I know you're ready for the full tea, so here it goes, I had become envious of Mama Bird because it seemed like she was freely able to function in all of the ways that God had also promised to me. He promised, but I was in what seemed like a perpetual holding pattern and there she was, getting to walk in what I felt like should be mine. Not that I felt that she shouldn't be walking in it; but I felt like I should be walking in it by now too. This woman that I had come to love and trust had now become a symbol of all of God's unfulfilled promises in my life. She is beautiful, married, has gorgeous children and she gets to walk in her ministry calling, seemingly without restraint. And here I am single, no kids, not even a spousal prospect and as for flowing freely in ministry? I feel like I am on the world's strongest, most stingy leash! In my mind, Mama Bird had become a painful reminder of all the discontentment I felt with God's plan and seeming lack of movement in my life.

Maybe that's not your story. Maybe your story is that you are single, or haven't been able to have children yet or you're working and waiting for a promotion and every time you log into IG, Snapchat and FB someone else is getting married, engaged, pregnant, promoted, and the list goes on and on. Maybe your story is that every time you see someone else getting what you want, you silently ask God,

"How did he get that promotion?" or

"Seriously?! She gets to get married and I'm still single?!" or "How is it that he found a good woman and I'm the 'good guy' who's still solo?!"

"How come she gets a new car and I'm still riding the bus?! She doesn't even tithe!"

"He's not even faithful!"

"They don't even deserve it!"

Be honest about what your story is. It will not be a pretty and scenic rabbit hole to go down, but unless you do and unless you properly identify this envy, it will eat you up from the inside out, leaving you bitter! We compare other people's opportunities, blessings, achievements and "stuff" because we are discontent with where we are in our own lives. We feel like they are walking around with our opportunities, blessings, achievements and "stuff."

"We compare other people's

opportunities, blessings, achievements and "stuff"

because we are discontent . . ."

Shall we revisit the revelation from the last chapter? God does not make mistakes. What's theirs is theirs and what's yours is yours. No one else can access what God's assigned to you. I'll prove it to you. Psalm 16:5 says, "Lord, You have assigned me my portion and my cup. You have made my lot secure."

Think of every door God has called you to walk through as being sealed with biometric security. No one else on earth can access the doors meant for you, except for you. God has made sure of it. So, when we see someone else with the things we want, our problem is not actually with them, our problem is with God and His plan. More specifically, our problem is that we have not fully submitted ourselves to God's plan. Perhaps we need to revisit chapter twelve, do not pass go and do not collect other people's things.

Sis… Bruh, if we're serious about living out this journey of surrender, we have to learn to call a spade a spade and deal with it appropriately. So, today, we are gonna deal with the envy that causes us to compare what we have and where we are in life to others. We're gonna resubmit our plans to God and accept His plans, and His timing, for our lives.

I know from experience that comparison can become so common that it seems like just a natural response; but just because it's become a habit, doesn't mean we can't break it. God would not have given us a directive to not envy if we were not able to do it. The problem is, we keep trying to do "God things" without God. "Huh?!" Yes, we keep trying to do what God requires, but in our own power. This indicates that our hearts are in the right place, but our minds are not yet. We think that we can carry out God's commands on our own. We think that if we can just muster up the will power, we can change ourselves and our behaviors for good.

We think that it's all on us to get it right, but, that was never God's intention. If we could "get it right" all on our own, God wouldn't have had to send Jesus, and Jesus wouldn't have had to send the comforter, the Holy Spirit. Check out John 14:15-16, it says, "If you love me, keep my commands. And I will ask the Father, and He will give you another advocate to help you and be with you forever." We've been trying to do this without using every tool in our arsenal. Make no mistake; the only way to be free from envy and comparison is to give up yours and everyone else's plans for you and surrender to God's plan. The only way to live in surrender is through the Holy Spirit. Let's pray...

Sincerely,
In Pursuit of Surrender

Prayer of Surrender: Comparison

Faithful Father,

You make no mistakes. Solidify that truth in my heart. It makes sense to my head, and I accept that truth with my mind, but I have yet to accept that truth in my heart. I confess that I have been giving into the sin of comparison. It's become second nature to me. But now I confess the root of my comparison habit, and it is that I don't trust You and I don't trust Your plan for me. Father, I'm so sorry. I'm sorry that I've trusted myself and my feelings more than You. I'm sorry that I've magnified Your plans for someone else and haven't surrendered to Your plans for me. I'm sorry for saying, with my actions and words, that You made a mistake when you made me, when you purposed me. I'm sorry for glorifying my own intellect over You.

I confess these things to You because it's You I've sinned against. But now, Father, I surrender my heart and my mind to You. I surrender my feelings to You. I surrender comparison to You. I lay down this need to look at other people and what they have and what they can do. Meet me here in my surrender and teach me to keep my eyes on You. Teach me to focus on You, what You are doing in my life and what You are saying for me. Teach me to listen for Your voice, especially when the enemy tries to stir up discontentment in my heart. Father, I pray that You would speak to me regarding Your plan for my life. Allow me to see where You are taking me, even if it's only a glimpse, so that I can get excited about what You are doing in me and stop focusing on what You are doing in others.

Teach me to celebrate what You are doing in others. Teach me to appreciate Your gifting in others as well as myself. Remind me, that no gift is better than another; they are all to bring You glory and to edify Your people. Teach me my identity in You. Teach me my purpose. Show me what You've equipped me with and train me to operate well in the giftings Your Holy Spirit has imparted.

Thank You in advance for meeting me here. I thank You that You've given me accountability to walk out this journey. I thank You that everything I ask according to Your will is done in the name of Jesus[45]. I thank You that You are delivering me from envy and teaching me how to love You and Your people better. And I thank You for never giving up on me. I pray this prayer in faith in the mighty and the matchless name of Jesus, Amen.

Sincerely,
In Pursuit of Surrender

---

[45] *1 John 5:14-15*

"God, I want to want you most…
But right now, I don't."

Surrendering My Desires
(11/26/18)

This chapter is not going to be easy. Not coincidentally, this will be one of those areas that you'll have to constantly surrender to God. At different moments of my life I've prayed prayers like the one above. Let me tell you of one such moment.

I had been in a relationship… No, let's call a spade, a spade. I was in a "situationship" and I had been for a couple of years. In retrospect, I was miserable with moments of happiness scattered throughout. I let the moments of happiness give me false hope that God would legitimize this "situationship" by agreeing to make him my husband.

Confused yet? Well, I was: hence the misery. Now, add to that ambiguity-fueled misery, spiritual turmoil and you've got the perfect storm. I was a saved woman in a "situationship." He and I had long since crossed physical boundaries. At this point, I was consistently giving husband privileges to someone who wasn't even officially my boyfriend, in title. Publicly, we told people that we were just friends. But, privately, we conducted ourselves like we were in an exclusive, committed relationship; and intimately, we treated each other like we had taken vows. Chiiiiiiiild, talk about confused!

Anyway, from the very beginning of this mess, God was telling me, "Aht aht! The answer is no."

But, stubborn, little ole' me, I forged onward! So, there I was, two and a half years, or so, in and I was in deep! This man was my first love. I loved him. I was in love with him. I was doing married things with him and praying desperately that God would make it right, make it okay, make it holy, make him my husband. God was adamant. The answer was, "No. Period." But, then it always had been, yet I was just now, at two and a half years in, coming to the realization that God wouldn't change His mind.

Simultaneously, I could increasingly hear God saying that He was calling me to greater. He had purpose for me, glorious purpose, but, I couldn't walk in that purpose until I let go of the "situationship." There I was, struggling with competing desires. I wanted this "relationship." I wanted this man more than I had ever wanted anything in my life. But, now, my curiosity was piqued... I wanted God too. I wanted to find out what He had to offer that could be better than this love I felt I'd found. So, one day, after one of our discipleship, small group studies (remember Mama Bird?), I had become very aware of these competing desires within myself. From that night, I began to pray very honestly,

"God, right now I want this 'relationship', but I also hear you saying that You've called me to greater. I want to walk in the fullness of Your calling, but, I also want this 'relationship.' Right now, I want this man more… But… I **want** to want You more."

It started with an honest prayer. I had competing desires and in that moment, without realizing it, what I actually did was surrender my desires to God for the first time.

In the years since, I've had to surrender my desires countless times. What that's looked like, for the most part, is, now that I'm in a place where my desires are in line with God's plans for me[46,] I have to surrender the weight of my desires to God. I find that although my desires are in line with God's plans, my timing is hardly ever in line with His. Meanwhile, as I wait for my desires to align with the timing of God's plans, I find that if I'm not careful, my desires can become my focus instead of God being my focus with those things being a happy byproduct. The danger of this is that I run the risk of wanting God's hand more than His presence, and those are dangerous waters. So, what's the surefire way to ensure that these desires don't become the focus of my pursuit? The answer is to constantly surrender them to God.

---

[46] See *Psalm 37:4*

Today, let's make the decision to not be led by our desires. Let's take a moment to investigate our motives to see if we are following and obeying God in order to recoup the benefits, or because we love Him and want deeper relationship with Him.

I challenge you to spend some time examining your desires. What is your predominant pursuit when you wake up in the morning? Are you chasing money to fund the lifestyle you desire? Are you chasing a man or a woman because they fit your plan? Are you chasing yourself, meaning, you wake up with the singular focus of pleasing yourself? Is there something in your life that is competing for first place? God is meant to be the greatest desire of our hearts, but is He? It's okay if your answer to that question, right now, is 'no.' It's okay because now you're aware. And what you now know is that God can handle the truth of competing desires in your heart. All He's waiting for is your surrender.

So, today let's discuss those competing desires with our accountability partners and lay them at God's feet; because, I can promise you, from experience, that from the moment you surrender your desires, God is working in your heart before you even realize it.

Sincerely,
In Pursuit of Surrender

*"In her deep anguish Hannah prayed to the Lord
weeping bitterly."*
~1 Samuel 1:10

Surrendering Hurt Feelings
(11/28/18)

As I've shared earlier in the book, I've occasionally come to the place of wanting to give up on God. It's a dark, desolate, hurting place. Although I've been there a few times before, it had never been quite as bad as this last time. Two months ago (at the time of this writing), I was struggling. I was coming face to face with the truth that I was desperately longing for a different type of connection. I was seeking God for understanding. You see, I've got great family and friends. I have really rich and fulfilling relationships and as for my relationship with God, more than ever before, I'm spending substantive time in His presence and hearing His voice and receiving revelation regularly. I experience His presence in powerful, life-changing ways; yet, I realized that I was longing for connection and never was it more apparent than the countless times a day when I hit the Facebook and Instagram icons on my phone screen. Each time I pressed one of those buttons, I literally felt an immediate emptiness rise up. I mean, it was so tangible that I felt like I could vomit a black hole from the pit of my stomach! Yet, no matter how many times I felt the pull of that black hole, I kept clicking those buttons. I realized that I had been feeling this way for weeks. I analyzed why I was feeling this and why I kept clicking time after time — scrolling, time after time. Finally, I realized that I was searching for connection, hoping someone would comment on one of my posts so that we could converse in a series of GIFs, Memes, Emojis and witty quips. I'd get my temporary fix, but when I came down from the high, the black hole was still there, sucking joy and energy and life right out of me. So, I'd click again, looking for another hit.

Finally, I decided to face the root of my click and scroll habit. I decided to acknowledge and surrender the emptiness and longing for connection. I prayed that God would help me understand where it was coming from and how to surrender it. Then I reached out to my accountability partner. I told her what was going on and how I'd surrendered it in prayer. As we texted back and forth, she asked me if I was currently fasting. Well, what did she ask that for?! I had prayed several hours ago by that point in our text conversation. I had surrendered it in prayer, but as my day went on I got heavier, not lighter. Nevertheless, I kept right on trucking along because there was work to be done. However, when she asked me that question, I immediately rolled my eyes and put my phone back in my pocket. Since I knew what her question meant and what response my answer would yield, I opted not to answer just then. You see, because, my answer was that I was not currently fasting, and she would then respond that, perhaps I should fast in order to get the clarity I was seeking from God.

I played the entire scenario out in my head until I became sufficiently annoyed. I finally texted her back three words, "No. I'm not." I had hoped that she would pick up on the double entendre:

1) No, I'm not currently fasting and
2) No. I'm not going to fast again.

I secretly hoped that somehow the sentiment with which I texted would reach her and stave off the inevitable................. It did not.

Sure enough, she suggested fasting. Then it happened. Out of nowhere, Jean Grey became Phoenix[47] For those less versed in the X-men Universe, I snapped! The dam broke! The last straw broke the camel's back and every other bone in its

---

[47] Jean Grey and Phoenix are different sides of the same character from the X-Men movies. Jean Grey is a powerful telekinetic mutant. Phoenix has been depicted in the movie series as the mutant that Jean Grey ultimately becomes. Phoenix is incredibly powerful, yet incredibly volatile and uncontrollable.

body! If this were a cartoon, my eye would've started twitching uncontrollably. The fat lady sang, then screamed, then stormed off the stage and exited the concert hall! Of course, this all happened internally because I was still at the church working dutifully to setup for an event.

I calmly walked to and fro, setting up decorations and moving furniture, but inside I was screaming at God. "How dare you! How dare you ask me to fast, again! Haven't I done everything You asked?! Haven't I faithfully waited and surrendered and waited some more?! Haven't I sought You?! Haven't I cried enough tears?! And You ask me to fast AGAIN?!?! FOR WHAT?! What did it get me the last time I fasted at your invitation?! Another promise that You haven't delivered on yet, THAT'S WHAT! NO! I'm not playing Your game anymore! I'm done with You! How dare you!!!" Deep breath… Yeah… Those were the actual things I was thinking.

Then… as I screamed these words in my mind, something happened. My anger gave way to the real culprit, pain. I was hurting. My words changed.

"How could you? How could You leave me here? I've been following You in faith all of this time and now You're just leaving me here in this darkness? In this valley? How could You say you love me and still leave me in this valley of perpetually unfulfilled promises? You should've never made me a promise if

You weren't going to keep it. Why would You get my hopes up to leave me here? How could you possibly love me and treat me like this?! How could you?"

During this time of brokenness, God used my accountability partner to comfort me; first, with her presence and then with words of encouragement. I was in anguish. I was the Shunammite woman in 2 Kings 4:8-37. I was Hannah. That was a Friday night. By the end of worship on Sunday, God had convicted my heart and called me to fast. He issued a challenge, and I issued one back.

"Fine. I'll give You one week, God."

I'm not saying I was right. I'm not saying it was wise. I'm just telling you the truth. I was still raw. I was still very much in my feelings, but I was now willing to meet God in fasting and prayer whether I felt like it or not. Welp... One week was more than He needed to show all the way up. From the first day I fasted, He began to give me unprecedented revelation that met me right where I was and gave me exactly what I needed to press on... perspective.

One of my absolute favorite places in all of scripture is 1 Samuel, chapter one. Now, while this is not where God took me during that week of fasting, I am now reminded of this passage.

I've often wondered, as I've read this text time and time again; what was different for Hannah in this chapter of her life than in every previous chapter?

How did things change for her here? Why did God not move until that moment, for her? As I revisited this, oh so familiar, passage, God gave me the answers to those questions. One of the things He showed me was that part of the reason Hannah's story changed here after years and years of the same is because Hannah finally did something different. In 1 Samuel 1:9, there is one all-important word. The verse says, "Once when they had finished eating and drinking in Shiloh, Hannah stood up..." I love this sentence so much and I'll tell you why. Context. That's right; I love this sentence so much because of the context. Check this out, in verses 1-8 of 1 Samuel, the writer introduces us to Hannah. We are told in the first couple of verses two important bits of information:

1) Hannah is one of two wives of Elkanah, an Ephraimite (Let's call him Nah Nah) and
2) Peninah (Nah Nah's other wife) has children, but Hannah has none.

Now, first of all, we can make some inferences based on the historical context of this account. What we know about this dispensation of time is that, culturally, probably the most important contribution of women in society was the bearing of children, especially male children. This was such an important contribution that if a woman were barren, she was considered cursed. She could very possibly be the talk of the town and not for good reasons. So, the very first thing the writer tells us is that Hannah is married to Nah Nah, and the very next thing we're told is that she can't have children.

As verses 1-8 continue, we now get a more full picture of Hannah's circumstances. We get to see that Peninah (Let's call her Penny because her character tells us she ain't worth much.) is a fertile jerk-face, but Nah Nah loves him some Hannah and just wants to see her happy. We learn that year after year, especially when it was time for the family to go up to Shiloh to worship God, Penny began with her taunts and ridicule. She literally ridiculed Hannah for something that Hannah had no control over, but desired so deeply. Every year Penny ridiculed and provoked Hannah to depression. She'd stop eating, and nothing could make her happy, not her husband, not his love and not his gifts. Every year it was the same story. Suddenly, we get to verse 9 and the writer says that all-important word, "Once." When we read verse 9, we recognize that the writer is giving us a literal picture of what happened; however, in my beautifully right-brained mind, I can't help but also see the figurative picture being painted.

For years and years Hannah has been taking Penny's abuse lying down. Oh, but when we get to verse 9… If I were to give a figurative paraphrase, I would say, "But this one time… At Shiloh… Hannah finally stood up for herself." She was tired of the same old thing, so this one time, instead of being provoked to depression, she tried something else.

We're talking about hurt feelings so let me connect the dots. Hannah was hurting. This was not some "I got a cut and need a Band-Aid" hurt; no, this was "years and years of being called cursed, inferior and useless" hurt. What's more, the scripture tells us that God was the one who had closed Hannah's womb. Hannah was beyond hurt, she was in constant anguish, for years. I don't know about you, but I don't have to imagine what it's like to be hoping and waiting and praying for something for years and hear God say, "No." or "Not yet." Then add to that pain, the pain of years of being ridiculed for God's "No" or "Not yet." Then add to that the pain of years of feeling "less than," cursed and avoided by others and we begin to see Hannah's anguish more clearly. She was hurting and rightfully so. She wanted to do what God commanded, "Be fruitful and multiply," but God, himself, had closed her womb and made her unable to do what He said…yet. And, so, every year Hannah internalized that hurt. It ate her up from the inside out. But, all it took was for Hannah to do something different one time. Just this one time she decided that internalizing her "hurt feelings" wasn't working, and she needed to take a stand and change her approach. This time, instead of turning her emotions inward, she chose to turn them upward. By changing her methodology, she set into motion the very miracle she'd been praying for, for years!

Now, there is so much more that precedes the manifestation of Hannah's miracle, but we'll save that for another time. What I want to focus on is how Hannah's miracle started — with her surrendering her hurt feelings.

Hannah had every right to be hurt, and maybe you do too. I don't know what that person said to you. I don't know what they did to you, what they took from you or who they took from you; but the pain is still there. Maybe you're angry with God because you feel like he took something or someone from you that was so dear to your heart. Maybe you're hurt because you feel like all you hear is "No," from God and it seems like He's withholding everything you want.

Whatever your pain, at some point you checked in, but never checked back out. You are still living in that place of pain. You have taken up residence in Heartbreak Hotel when it was only meant to be a temporary stay. What you may not realize is that holding onto this pain is holding you back from experiencing the fullness of God's joy and plan for your life; and if you refuse to let go of these hurt feelings, they could fester into a wound (more about that in the next chapter).

So, I'm challenging you… No, God is challenging you to let go of these hurt feelings that are holding you back from living, from loving, from serving, from soaring. I would give you a moment right now to just feel what you feel before surrendering, but God says, "You've held onto those feelings for far too long. It's time to let it go like Elsa!"

This is normally the place where we would dig into a prayer of surrender, but read on to the next chapter. We'll do this "A Christmas Carol" style and show you the Ghost of Hurt Feelings Future, then we'll surrender it all at once.

Sincerely,
In Pursuit of Surrender

"Time doesn't heal wounds. It doesn't have the power to do that...Only God, The True Healer, can."

Surrendering My Wounds
(12/4/18)

You've been stabbed! You look down at your blood-stained hands and fall to the ground. Right before you blackout, you see flashing lights approaching. Your final thought before passing out is,

"An ambulance. I'm saved."

When you awaken, you are in more pain than before you passed out. You realize that you're in a hospital room, but when you look down you see that you've bled right through your hospital gown. You press the nurse's button and when your nurse arrives you tell him that you think your stitches have broken open. He looks puzzled and says, "I'll be right back." He ducks out and reappears a moment later with your doctor. When she asks, 'How are you feeling?" You tell her you're in pain and you think that you busted your stitches. She chuckles, "Stitches? You don't have stitches."

"What?! Why not?!" You ask in confusion.

"We're waiting," she says, matter-of-factly.

"Waiting?! Waiting for what? I'm losing blood and I feel worse than I did before I came here!"

She smiles and tells you, "We're waiting for your wound to heal."

"So, you haven't started treatment?!" You inquire in frantic disbelief.

"Calm down. You'll work yourself up for nothing. Here, we believe that time heals all wounds, so it's just a matter of time before you're ready to be discharged," she chimes chipperly before heading for the door.

"Wait, what?! I'm dying!!! I need help!"

Right before walking out, the doctor turns and non-chalantly chides, "Don't be so dramatic. You'll be fine, in time. You'll see."

She leaves. Your nurse leaves. Shortly after, you start sweating and shivering all at the same time. Now, it's not just your stab wound in your left abdomen that's hurting, the entire left side of your body is hurting. Your wound is infected. You have a fever. The nurses keep walking right past your room. When they actually do stop in, they do nothing, except to remind you that time heals all wounds. But, time runs out. You die; and when the doctor comes back she covers you with a sheet. The nurse asks why time didn't heal your wound and she says, "She/He must not have wanted healing enough. You've gotta really want to be healed."

Sound familiar; minus the knife wound and the most unethical, non-Hippocratic-oath-taking hospital staff ever, of course? How many times have you been told that time heals all wounds? That is one of the most damaging clichés in life and I think it is well past time to retire it! It. Is. A. LIE! Time doesn't heal wounds. It doesn't have the power to do that. But, the God, who stands outside of time, can. Telling people that time will heal their wounds is as asinine as that sorry excuse for a hypothetical doctor telling you that your hypothetical, gaping knife wound would heal in time. Time doesn't heal wounds. It can't! Only God, The True Healer, can. So, can we agree to stop perpetuating this crock of crap?! Great! Now that that's handled, let's move on.

There's a reason why I chose to go through the last chapter and this chapter together, before going to God in a prayer of surrender. The correlation is that if you refuse to deal with your hurt feelings, they can become wounds that alter and affect your behaviors, your thought processes, your relationships and even your ability to walk in the fullness of your calling.

Many of us are walking around with wounds, and we don't even realize it. Others have wounds and are in denial. Still others of us are aware of our wounds but "refuse to let them stop us." The problem is… They are stopping us. We may achieve and accomplish some things in life despite and sometimes in light of our wounds, but the truth is, if we don't allow God to heal our wounds, we will never be functioning at full capacity. We will never fully be who we are called to be, let alone accomplish all that we were meant to accomplish. You have to decide if you'll settle for a piece of promise or if you want to walk in the fullness of God's promise, purpose and plan. As for me, I've made a decision. Let me tell you another story. I must, though, very seriously include a trigger warning. There is no graphic detail here, but this story alludes to sexual abuse.

There was a little girl who was no more than eight years old. She was growing up in a poor, single-parent household. She was shy and quiet and constantly bullied. This beautiful little brown girl, let's call her Beautiful Brown, who didn't know her own beauty or destiny, had an uncle who had been on drugs. Once, when her mom was at work, this uncle sent this beautiful brown girl upstairs after sending her little sister and cousin outside to play. Once upstairs, he told Beautiful Brown to take off her clothes. He did obscene and perverse things to this beautiful girl. When Beautiful Brown told her mother what happened, her mother believed her; extended, family did not. Beautiful Brown and her beautiful mama were called liars. For all of her ordeal, Beautiful Brown received the "gift" of low self-esteem.

Eventually, this uncle went to prison for drug charges. He was in prison for years until this beautiful brown girl became a beautiful brown pre-teen with low self-esteem. She believed she was unloved no matter how much family said they loved her. On the day that uncle was released from prison, all the family came together to celebrate. Beautiful Brown was very uncomfortable about seeing uncle again, so she didn't go into the house to celebrate. She stayed in her mom's car because sitting alone in a car in a parking lot in the dark seemed safer for her than facing uncle.

Beautiful Brown's grandmother, uncle's mother, was unhappy with her decision to stay in the car, so she came to the car and reprimanded Beautiful Brown for hurting uncle's feelings. She then made Beautiful go inside and celebrate uncle, the man who stole her innocence and self-worth. For all her hard work, Beautiful Brown was given the "gifts" of self-loathing and never trusting her own instincts, even if they were correct.

Beautiful Brown became a beautiful grown woman who not only hated herself and her life, but also felt unloved and unworthy of love, and she still didn't know that she was beautiful. She was wounded long before she made it out of childhood. Did Beautiful Brown have a right to be hurt and remain wounded?

Yes. Yes, I did. Thankfully, I serve the Beautiful God that loved me too much to let me just remain that beautiful, brown, broken and wounded girl turned woman. That wasn't my name, and He refused to let me spend my life answering to it.

Once, when I was a teenager, we were having our weekly healing and deliverance service at my childhood church. As I received prayer, the minister said that God was calling me to forgiveness. In that moment, I knew exactly who it was that I needed to forgive. I had the right to be hurt and angry, but the hurt, anger and rage that I was living with was exacerbating this wound that was growing inside, unbeknownst to me. In that moment, as a teenager, I made an impossible decision to forgive the man who hurt me. I forgave him, and I meant it. I felt a weight lift off of me.

Fast forward to 2017. I was a completely different woman than the one I had become almost seven years prior. You see, the woman I had become by 2010 was being led almost exclusively by her brokenness. I wasn't aware of it, but my life, my behavior, my relationships and my choices were all being controlled by the wound that was left in the wake of a tumultuous childhood. But, by 2017, God had worked strategic and intensive healing in me and I was a completely different person; Thank God! You know who wasn't a completely different person? That's right. You guessed it... uncle.

Uncle was then fifty-seven years old, back to his old drug and alcohol habits and using as many people as would allow him. My mom, being the tender heart that she was, did not want to see her brother living on the street when he lost his apartment, so she once again let him stay with her. He was there for months and seemed to be doing okay. Then he and his girlfriend stole majorly from my mother. He was disinvited.

Then, weeks later, while mom was out of town visiting family, uncle kicked in her front door to gain access to the apartment where he was no longer welcome. I was so far beyond livid that all of the hatred and disgust that I had forfeited over the last years, when I had chosen to forgive him, came rushing back all at once. I was heavy with the weight of woundedness. Sixteen years of unforgiveness that I had previously forgone all came back. Talk about livid. I had forgiven him, let God do extensive work in my heart and uncle got to keep skating through life using people like toilet paper and being the same bacteria-spreading parasite that he was twenty-something years ago(that's truly how I felt, y'all)?!

When God saw this building in me, He met me right in the midst of it. One Wednesday night in 2017 as we were having our staff prayer at Macedonia (my current church home), God blew through the room something fierce and used folks that had no idea what was building up on the inside of me to call it out. God came through our staff prayer in the most unexpected way and began to call for forgiveness. There were several folks who had been holding onto some unforgiveness. It was eating away at us. At first, I won't lie, I was resistant. I kept telling myself, "I forgave him years ago. God can't be talking about me." Then God turned up the heat and I knew that it was me He was talking to as well.

The truth is that I had withdrawn my forgiveness when uncle had proven to be the same person from all those years ago. Uncle had ripped off the scab of my wound and there it was, infection festering. I thought I was done with all that, but I still had a wound that God was healing and in order for this wound to heal properly and completely, God had to let the scab be ripped off just one more time to expose the still-sore root of the wound. Uncle had ripped off the scab with his actions, then months later, during prayer, I ripped off the Band-Aid that I had slapped on my gaping wound. I had forgiven him once, but that night I forgave him once and for all. Then, at God's leading, I prayed one of the hardest prayers that I've prayed in my entire life. I prayed for restoration in uncle's life. I prayed that he would surrender his life to God in earnest and be used for God's purpose. I released him from all the wrong he'd done to me and those that I loved. I didn't want to. I didn't feel like it. But, I knew it was necessary, so, I forgave him. End of the story, right?... Don't I wish.

Fast forward to early 2018. I was leading praise and worship at a conference when God moved so powerfully through the ministry of Apostle Ebony J. Williams of Equally Yoked Ministries. She shared her testimony of how God had delivered her from the spirit of perversion that, in her, had manifested as homosexuality. She spoke about how the spirit could manifest in different ways in different people. She began to run down the list of ways that the spirit of perversion can manifest and then, with the pin-point precision of a Black Ops sharpshooter, she fired the three shots that rocked me to my core. Her words rang out and reverberated in my spirit: "… lust, pornography, masturbation…" Now, I know at this point you're wondering if I've gotten off the beaten path, but stick with me a little longer. You see, that's how wounds work; everything is unconnected until it's not anymore. In that moment God began to connect the dots.

At that point, I already had some knowledge of soul ties and how they work; a few months prior to this conference, I had come across evidence of what other sins uncle had been indulging. Care to take a guess what they were? … You got that right, lust, pornography and masturbation.

Guys let me be so clear about what I say next. Demons do not care about your age or preserving your innocence. They don't care if you are eight or eighty. If you have purpose in the Kingdom of God, and we all do, then there is a bounty on your head. I'll tell you how I know. After this conference I began to learn even more about soul ties. As I internalized the information I found, I began to reflect on my own childhood and dot after dot was connected until I could see the whole picture. Here's the ugly truth: I have been struggling against lust, pornography and masturbation since I was a young child... after the sexual abuse. Now, there are those who deny or are unsure the existence of demons and soul ties. I'm not interested in debating their existence; I'm sharing what I know of them, from experience.

Soul ties are an interesting and dangerous thing and while sex isn't the only mode of transmission, it is a common, and most efficient one. This is why God intended for the gift of sex to be unwrapped within the protection and covenant of marriage. All it takes is to lie down one time with someone to get up with everything with which they're struggling and have made covenant. Soul ties open the doors for spiritual activity whether we realize it or not. The really jive thing is that you don't even have to engage in consensual sexual activity in order for soul ties to form. Even when the act is non-consensual—rape, molestation, abuse—soul ties are formed. Here I am, thirty-something and finally coming to the realization that this battle I've been fighting since childhood, against these sins often too taboo to share with anyone else, is actually not "my fight." When uncle molested me, he had formed an unhealthy and unholy soul tie that left me vulnerable and fighting against the spirits with which he made covenant.

I was internally enraged. Not only did I have to fight low self-esteem, learn to trust myself, learn to forgive him and then learn to forgive myself; you mean to tell me that some of the spiritual battles I was currently fighting were ones I'd inherited from him?! Forced on me?! Well, now I'm just plain ole' pissed off! Are you kidding me?! All of this goes back to the same wound?!

"How could I be leading worship and struggling with these sins?

What would people think?"

Yyyyyyyyup; and at the root of this wound was an unhealthy soul tie that I never asked for, I never wanted and for most of my life, was unaware. As an adult, understanding my actions, I was so ashamed that I could not overcome the triad. I hadn't told anyone about my struggle. How could I be leading worship and struggling with these sins? What would people think? Then, God gave me understanding and perspective to know that I don't have to be ashamed anymore. Besides, if I don't talk about it, who will? God's people experiencing freedom is way more important than my pride and reputation. So, we're gonna talk about it.

After that conference, God continued to connect the dots. These sins that I'd been fiercely battling since childhood were the product of this soul-tie at the heart of this wound I'd been carrying around. With this soul tie, the spirit of perversion was given entry, legal rights, to enter my life and wreak havoc without my permission and knowledge. It became clear that if I wanted to be whole and free, I had to destroy the soul-tie that was keeping this wound alive and poisoning my life. So, I went to war and broke that tie. In so doing, I got rid of the infection that had caused this wound to fester in me. After years of being wounded, I was free to heal.

What I also learned through this process is that, much like love, forgiveness is a conscious and ongoing decision. I had forgiven uncle as a teen, then again in 2017 and then new evidence surfaced that further upset me but I had to make the continual decision to forgive him. Just as God does for us. Jesus died on the cross for every sin—past, present and future. Therefore, in the face of this new evidence against uncle, I refused to walk down the path of unforgiveness again. Now, I've also learned the beauty and necessity of forgiveness without reconnection, but, this newfound freedom, this deliverance, all started with my willingness to surrender my wound.

I don't know what your wound is. Maybe it's the wound from an absent, emotionally distant or abusive father. Maybe, it's a wound from a bitter, spiteful or abusive mother. Maybe, it's a wound from years of bullying. Perhaps it's a wound of grief because you felt someone was taken from you way too soon or a wound from a bad relationship that left you broken and jaded. Whatever your wound, you probably do have the right to be hurt and upset; but God has so much more for you than a future that's progressively dimmed and perpetually deferred by the pain and anger of the past.

I know they hurt you. You have the right to be hurt; but, you also have the right and the invitation to be healed because that is what you deserve. Not because I say so, but because God does. Stop letting your wounds keep you from your destiny.

God wants you to begin healing those wounds that have stunted your growth and held you back from purpose and destiny. You may be hesitant because you may not even want to extend forgiveness to those who've wounded you, but don't let that stop you from starting the process today. God can handle the truth. It's okay to let Him know that you want healing, but you're not ready to forgive yet. It's okay to tell God that you just don't know how to forgive someone who left such a lasting wound. God just needs a heart that is willing to let Him do His work; and trust that He will teach you to forgive at the right moment. Just, please, don't put off the healing process any longer. I am pleading with you. God has so much He wants to do through you; but, first, He needs access to do work in you. Consider this, there is someone in this world with that same wound and God wants to use you to show them that healing is possible. He wants to use your story to help teach them how to receive healing; but, their healing starts with your surrender.

Today is not going to be the easiest of days because we're getting ready to pray that God would help us take inventory by revealing those wounds we've been hiding, ignoring and suppressing. We are going to pray that God would prep our hearts for surgery, then we're going to give Him permission to go into those wounded, infected, inflamed, painful places and begin to heal us. Time doesn't heal wounds. It can't. Only our Father, The Healer, can.

Today… Right at this moment, you have a choice. Are you going to keep being hurt and stay exactly where you are or are you going to give up this hurt to the one who can repair the damage and move you toward His purpose and plans for you? Me? I choose surrender. I refuse to let anything keep me from everything that God has planned and purposed for my life. There are lives attached to my obedience… and yours. So, what do you choose? Let's surrender it to Him today.

Sincerely,
In Pursuit of Surrender

A Heart That Forgives
(6/20/19)

As you go into your prayer time today, I'm gonna ask that you first listen to the song A Heart That Forgives by Kevin Levar and One Sound. I've placed this song, as well as others referenced in this book, in a playlist on multiple streaming platforms and I encourage you to visit page 259 at the back of this book to find out where you can stream this playlist. This song, in particular, is powerful from beginning to end, but my absolute favorite lyrics of the song are:

> *"...Just like your Son*
> *I give up my right*
> *To hold it against them*
> *With hatred inside..."*

Stunning, isn't it, this contrast of an innocent Jesus hanging on a cross cruelly forced on Him vs. us being hurt by others. Jesus had a right to hold it against every one of them... every one of us. Instead, in the moments before He gave up His life, Jesus prayed, "Father, forgive them, for they know not what they do." He gave up His right to hold their sin against them, to hold it against us! That's the same thing God is asking of us in this moment, to give up our right to hold these wrongs against those who've hurt us.

We have a right. It's legitimate, but, it's hurting us. It's killing us. As you listen to this song, I encourage you to listen and hear every single word allow them to minister to you as you prepare to go to God and surrender your wounds and all of your hurt feelings that are on their way to becoming wounds? Although it seems repetitive, there's something especially powerful that happens towards the end. If you listen carefully, you get to hear what this surrender, this forgiveness really looks like — where it starts. It starts with a heart-cry. It starts with being honest about where you are. It starts in prayer. So, let's get to it…

Sincerely,
In Pursuit of Surrender

"Sometimes I've gotta stop
Remember that you're God
And I am not, so
Thy will be done…"
~Hilary Scott, Thy Will

Surrendering "Them"
(1/22/19)

I am a helper, a natural nurturer and a natural sacrificial lover. When I love people, I want to do everything in my power to help and support them. When I love people, I can be very protective of them. I don't take kindly to people hurting the people that I love. Now, thankfully, over the years, God has taken the time to conform my character to His; oh, but once upon a time—about seven years ago (at the time of this writing)—my baby sister (remember her from before?... "But you're my role model.") was in an abusive relationship. When I caught wind of it, I immediately sprang into Mama Bear Mode. This dude was so psychologically, emotionally and verbally abusive to my sister that I wanted to do him physical harm. Part of me wanted to harm him because of the hurt he was causing her, but the other part of me wanted to harm him because of the pain that I knew was still to come since he was following the textbook pathology of an abuser. I cried. I prayed.

I asked for prayer from others because there was a rage building on the inside of me every time I spoke to her and learned a little bit more. This was not a happy time. Almost everything in me wanted to drive hundreds of miles to my sister and snatch her out of that situation; however, if you know anything about the dynamics of an abusive relationship, sometimes, that's the worst thing that you can do. The Holy Spirit became my counselor during that time. He began to show me that her deliverance (and my peace) would come when I learned to let go. Now, hear me when I say that God told me to let go, not to walk away. I did it. It was one of the most difficult things I've ever done, but I had to. I needed to. Once I did, everything changed... but it didn't change right away.

As I reflect on that time, it was then that God was teaching me how to surrender my "them." We all have a "them," you know, the people we would kill a brick and make a rock bleed over. We all have at least one person that has our heart in such a way that if someone wanted to meet Jesus, all they would have to do is hurt that one person and we would personally arrange the meeting.

"Why is this even a 'thing,' Ange? Why would I need to let go of someone that I love?"

This entire book is about a process—our process, and what it looks like to walk out the process of surrender. But, what if I told you that each time you step in and become the savior for that person(s), you're robbing God of the chance to be God in their life. You're robbing them of the chance to walk through their own process with God. You're robbing them of the chance to fall in love with God. You're robbing them of the chance to start or deepen their relationship with God because you keep showing up, thus, for them, you've become God.

I am not telling you to cut people off. I am saying that we need to be seeking God for wisdom. Sometimes God is asking us to lay off and let Him do what He wants to do, but we're too busy being in rescue mode that we miss His instruction. The truth is, every calling is not our calling. If we are going to be who God called us to be and do all that God called us to do, then we have to be okay with not doing what He has not called us to do. I know it's not the easiest thing in the world, but it is immensely helpful for me when I remind myself that He is God. Because He's God, I can rest assured that He has a plan for him, for her, for "them", just like for me.

Nothing escapes the scope of God's sovereignty; and sometimes, He chooses to use us, but sometimes He is creating an opportunity for someone else to step up. Still other times He wants to be the one to miraculously deliver. But, if I'm always stepping in, if I'm never listening for His lead, I may be stunting their growth and stressing me out, when God has called me to rest and watch Him do what He does.

God told me it was time to let go of baby girl, not to walk away. Whenever she called, I answered. I listened. My heart still broke a little more as I listened to her cry. Then I listened for God's voice and spoke what He spoke. I took every chance to point her back to Him. I reminded her, that God loved her and that He was waiting to hear her voice again in prayer. I prayed with her. I prayed over her. I prayed for her and as I prayed, I found peace. As I prayed, He ministered to her heart. As I prayed, He shifted the atmosphere. Yes, I let go of her, but only because I knew she was in His hands. In due time, God, not I, showed her when it was time to get out. When she called me to help, He released me to go get baby girl… and her two beautiful babies. Yet, her deliverance didn't come until I stopped trying to figure out how to rescue her and released her to the only one who could deliver.

Who is your "them"? Maybe you're not swooping in to save someone at every turn, but maybe you're worrying yourself sick about them every day. Maybe you're badgering them about a relationship with God. Maybe you're beating them over the head with scripture trying to get them "on the right path," and it's only pushing them farther away. God says,

"Open your hands and release them to me. The reason you're not seeing the result you want is that you're out of place. You're out of position. You're out of order. You come and lay them at the altar, time and time again, and when you're done crying and praying to me, you pick them back up and carry them right back with you."

He says, "Open your hands and surrender them to me, once and for all, and watch me do, in months, what you couldn't do in years." God is asking us to give "them" up and rest knowing that they are in the most capable hands that will ever hold them— His.

Some six or seven years ago, God taught me how to let her go, which prepared me to let more of "them" go. There will always be a "them." But the good news is, there will always be Him. So, I'm challenging you today to take a step. If you're willing, even if you don't know how, we're going to pray and ask God to teach us to surrender our "them" into His almighty hands. Let's go to Him in prayer and let "them" go.

Sincerely,
In Pursuit of Surrender

"I'M not right! YOU'RE wrong!!"
(yyyyyyup. You read that correctly)
~Nobody Will Take Credit,
Just SMH (Shaking My Head)

Surrendering Pride
(1/22/19)

Have you ever been smack dab in the middle of a heated disagreement? You're making your point, they keep "side-stepping", so you raise your voice because "they must not have heard you the first time." Then they raise their voice because they're "petty" and "just don't want to understand you." Then it happens. It slapped you right in the face while their back was turned and you were… "educating" them even louder than the first two times you yelled… I mean, "said" it. You finished your "impassioned" speech and turned away waiting for their "obnoxious reply," and your mind started racing. Searching, "How can I end this argument right now?!" No, you're not finally trying to get to peace. You're not even tired of arguing yet. It's just that… in the middle of your last diatri… ummm, "rebuttal" you realized that you're actually… wrong. (*winces in pain*) I know! It sucks!! You're not just a little wrong, you're soooooooo wrong; and now you're aware of it, but, what are you gonna do?! You've been ranti… I'm mean, "sharing" on and on for the better part of the last hour and… "We'll just agree to disagree!!!" You interrupt, as you haphazardly toss the words over your shoulder like a no-look pass to the trash can and storm out of the room, slamming the door before they could get another word out.

You know the routine from here. You all only have essential conversation for the next two days, and by "essential conversation" I mean, a series of curt grunts, mostly accompanied with either dagger eyes or rolling eyes. "Mm," means yes. "Mm mm," means no; and a silent, direct stare, a la Auntie Maxine Waters means, "You better back up out my face 'cuz there's about to be some furniture moving; and although I love the Lord, you bouta catch these hands, forthwith… bruh!" That's a rough translation, but you get the gist. At some point, one of you is sufficiently out of your feelings enough to start some conversation. It begins with awkwardly stilted words and ends with a joke and the other smiles, but doesn't speak yet because there are strict rules of engagement in these Pridal Wars.

Here's the vital question, "Why?" Why do we continually go through this song and dance? In that moment when we realized we were wrong, why not just stop, admit it and apologize? I know; who does that, right?! But, you know who does that? People who have learned to surrender their pride, that's who. Let's be frank, what good thing has pride yielded us? Or, if I may pose the question like Ms. Jackson, what has pride done for you lately? I mean, truly. Pride does quite a few things, but none of them are particularly good. Pride isolates us, distorts our vision, separates us from reality, damages our relationships and keeps us from living and walking in all that God has called us to. Now this is not an exhaustive list, just a little something to get us started. Tell you what, I'll save us both time by not digging into all the ways that pride is keeping our relationships on life support. I'll just dig into some of the ways it's hindering our most important relationship—the one we have with God. After all, that relationship is the one that governs all the others.

Here's a quick history lesson. Throughout the Bible, from the Old Testament to the New Testament, we are reminded that pride is detestable to God, but humility delights Him. The very reason we were created was to worship God—to reflect His glory in all the world—and in doing so, to point the world back to Him.

Did you know that lucifer (little "l" 'cuz we put no "respeck" on his name) was originally the archangel who was tasked with worship in Heaven? Yeah! This dude was up in Heaven, made of gemstones that easily reflected God's glory. God created him in such a way that it would be easy for him to operate in his purpose—easy for lucifer to reflect God's glory; however, reflecting God's glory wasn't enough for luci. He decided that he didn't want to reflect God's image and bring God glory. Instead, he wanted the glory for himself, and that, ladies and gentlemen, is what got lucifer's tail handed to him before he was kicked out of Heaven... and his lil' friends too!

This dude became so tempted and overcome by pride that he rose up and attempted a coup in Heaven to try and overthrow the God who created him! The audacity! To actually rise up and attempt to dethrone the all-powerful God who created him and gave us... I mean him purpose! What is wrong with us?!... Him... us... You get the point, right?

You see, after the failed coup in Heaven, God created earth and all its inhabitants. Then, He created man and woman in His image and gave them dominion over the earth. Did you catch that? We were created to do what lucifer failed to do, to bear God's image and point back to Him. We were created to worship Him. Y'all, we took luci's spot; and he is maaaaaaddd. I'm not talking a little mad; he's big mad! That's why he's constantly trying to get us to fall into the same pride trap that he did. That's why the pride monster is so hard to shake. That's why we are inherently selfish. That's why we throw tantrums when we don't get our way. That's why we shake our fist toward Heaven when God tells us "No." That's why we have trouble trusting God and giving up control, thinking we know better—because of death, spelled P-R-I-D-E.

Pride isolates us from God. It literally causes us to see our teammate, our greatest ally, as our enemy. Before we know it, we're fighting against God instead of our true enemy. Pride causes us to glorify our own intellect and understanding rather than seek God for wisdom and understanding. Pride causes us to remain in a holding pattern longer than God intended because we refuse to give up our will, our plans and our desires for His. Pride will have us looking like a brand new bag of potato chips—more air than substance and a constant disappointment and annoyance to all who come in contact with it. Pride is not pretty. There are not artistic words to make it palatable. To state it as the Bible does, "Pride goes before destruction, a haughty spirit before a fall[48]." And, let me be further clear, the destruction of the prideful is rarely mourned by those who witness it. Pride is an ugly thing, and it has been holding us back long enough.

---

[48] *Proverbs 16:18*

"I want to be used for God's purposes. I want Him to get the glory . . ."

God has purpose, calling, anointing and promises for all who will humble themselves before Him in order to win the glory for Him. God wants to shake up this world and turn the hearts of men back to Him and He wants to use us to do it; however, God's plan will not be held hostage by prideful hearts that will not yield to Him. To put it plainly, God wants to use us, but He sure doesn't have to. God gives us a window, within which we can lay down our pride willingly. The alternative is Proverbs 16:18, we'll humble ourselves or be humbled by the fall.

I've made my decision. I'm gonna let God be God and remember that I am not. I want to be used for God's purposes. I want Him to get the glory through me. Therefore, today I choose to surrender pride — pride that has caused me to tantrum against God because I didn't get what I wanted, how I wanted, when I wanted. I'm done with trying to exercise control over situations because I think I know what's best. I surrender pride to God because I've seen where it ultimately leads. I've seen how it's interfered in my relationships and damaged those with whom I was in relationship. I've seen how pride isolated me and caused me to see my teammates as enemies. I've seen how it has held me back from purpose because I was too worried of what people would think if I were to fully be who God created. I've seen pride rob me of joyful moments because it led me to comparison instead. I have seen pride at work in me, but no more. God did not call me to be full of myself. Instead, He called me to be so full of Him that when the world looks at me, they see only God's reflection in me. That's what I'm after.

My hands are up. I'm done living for my own agenda, glory and pleasure. I recognize that this won't be a "one and done" surrender. This is an everyday surrender. Today I choose to keep surrendering and tomorrow, God willing, I'll wake up and choose surrender all over again. That's what I choose. What about you?

Sincerely,
In Pursuit of Surrender

"I've spent too much of my life trying to be what other people wanted. I'm only interested, now, in being who God created, and let the chips fall where they may."

Surrendering My "Not Enough"
A.K.A. The Fear Of Rejection
(1/22/19)

Let me just be clear right up front; a large part of the reason why it took me two entire years to write this book is that the entire time I've been writing, fear has been whispering to me.

I'd pull out my book, it whispered. I'd pull out my pen, it whispered. I'd start writing, it whispered. The next time I reached for my book, the whispers grew. The next time I thought about reaching for my book, the whispers reverberated. Sometimes I faced this fear head on and decided to write through the whispers. Other times, I conveniently became too "busy."

On New Year's Eve 2018 I looked this fear right in the face. I confessed to myself that I'd been fighting this thing all along and way too long. Then, I fell down at the altar and confessed it to God. It was… It is, fear of rejection and this time it came in the form of "not enough."

I will be transparent. I've heard God calling me to write and release books for years. He's confirmed it through prophetic words, in His Holy Word and in my spirit over and over and over and… at this point the Energizer Bunny ain't got nothin' on God. What kept me from starting for so many years were the thoughts that, "Nobody cares what I have to say. It's not like I'm that interesting or have much to say anyway. What if I write a book and nobody buys it? What if people read it and don't like it? … Don't like me? What if I'm not eloquent or articulate enough? What if… I'm not enough?"

But, I finally started writing a book, scared. I got halfway through and stopped because I didn't feel qualified enough to complete it. A year or so later, I started this book. I was writing, scared. I kept writing, scared. Every time I grabbed my book and pen the thoughts lingered, "What will people think? What will this person think? What will that person think?" I kept writing, scared. Fear or no fear, I kept writing. As I got to these last several chapters at the end of 2018, the voice got louder. It got harder and harder to pick up my book and pen, but I kept writing. Scared. But writing.

Then this past Sunday, January 20th, 2019, my Pastor, Brian J. Edmonds preached, "Do It Scared;" which was just the final push I needed—a reminder that, yes, fear of rejection is real and, yes, I've chosen to surrender it to God, but, a true lifestyle of surrender is about still performing while in the process. I've surrendered this fear of rejection, but the voice is still there, "What if I'm not enough?" But, while I wait and watch God work it out in the process, do you know what I'm doing? Exactly what God said. I'm writing scared, but I'm writing. I still wonder, "What if I'm not enough for the world."

But then I'm reminded, Jesus wasn't 'enough' for the world... until He was. Over the voice of fear, I now hear God saying:

> "Enough for the world?! You were never made for this world, Angelique. You were made to speak to it, command it, minister to it; but you were never made *for* it! Don't you ever forget that you were made for Me, and I am well pleased with you, daughter."

I've gotta tell you, the acceptance of the world means so much less when you're reminded that you have The Father's acceptance and when you remember that we aren't here for the world. We are sent to it, for His glory; and since it's for His glory, His approval is all that matters.

So, yeah, this surrendering of the fear of rejection is currently under construction, but that's the whole point of this pursuit of surrender: I'm always under construction, and I promise I will be surrendering until the day I die and then forever.

Sincerely,
In Pursuit of Surrender

EPILOGUE

Let me, please, reiterate that this book is not a "be all, end all." Once you've completed this book and walked through these pages in your own life, it's just the very tip of the iceberg. The truth is, if we are living this life correctly, every day that God wakes us, we'll be surrendering something. Maybe it'll be something new tomorrow. Maybe it'll be something you've surrendered before. Maybe it'll be a bit of both. The point is, if we are going to live this life in the way that God intended, then we are going to spend every single day surrendering to Him. Surrender doesn't stop at a certain age. With surrender, you never "arrive"; you are only ever pursuing. No one said it would be easy; that's why this book didn't come with an easy button. But, it will be worth it.

I pray that God gives each and every one of you who have read this book humility to admit that you can't do this alone, courage to surrender even when it doesn't feel good and faith to keep pressing even when you can't see the payoff. I pray that your relationship with God would grow beyond the desire for God's promises and transform into a desire for HIM and a love solely based on who He is. I pray that this book would spark an eternal flame of surrender in your heart, and I pray that flame would ignite a movement to take this world back for The Kingdom of God.

I have many family members (my brothers, sisters-in-love, aunts, uncles, cousins) who have served in the Armed Forces of the United States of America. To them I'd like to take a quick moment to say, "Thank you." From the bottom of my heart, thank you for your bravery, your sacrifice, your strength and for coming back home. To those who are reading this who have served in the Armed Forces, thank you. If you have family who served, thank you. If you've lost family in the Armed Forces, thank you for your sacrifice; you have my deepest respect, sympathy and condolences.

Many of the branches of the military have mottos, sayings that help remind them and the rest of the world of that for which they stand, of what they believe, of who they are.

If I were in the US Navy I might say
"Semper Fortis,: which means "Always Strong" or "Always Courageous."

If I were in the US Air Force I might say,
"Aim High... Fly-Fight-Win."

If I were in the US Army I might say,
"This we'll defend."

If I were in the US Coast Guard I might say, Semper Paratis, which means, "Always Ready."

If I were in the US National Guard I might say, "Always Ready, Always There."

If I were a US Marine I might say, Semper Fidelis (or Semper Fi), which means "Always Faithful" or "Always Loyal."

But, I'm not in the Armed Forces of the United States of America. My citizenship is in Heaven and I serve in the Lord's Royal Armed Forces; therefore, what I would say might seem counterintuitive from a military standpoint, but isn't that just like our God to use the foolish things to confound the wise?[49] You see, in the Lord's Army our motto is, Semper Tradentes, which means "Always Surrendering," or "Always Yielding." Let that become not just your life's motto, but your heart's cry. Let that become the pursuit of your life; always surrender to God because our surrender is the only way to win this fight.

Sincerely,
Forever In Pursuit of Surrender
Semper Tradentes
Angelique A. Strothers

---

[49] *1 Corinthians 1:27*

"Stop Fighting.

Start Surrendering.

Boo—yah."

(Ooo-rah was already taken. *Shrugs*)

The Prayer of Salvation

If you've never prayed a prayer of salvation and would like to give your life to Christ, I am going to ask that you pray this prayer out loud as Romans 10:9 says that if we confess with our mouths that Jesus is Lord and believe in our hearts that God raised Him from the dead, then we will be saved. Welcome to the family! If you already have relationship with God, please feel free to use this prayer as a tool as God may use you to lead others to Christ.

Prayer of Salvation

Dear God,

I confess that I am a sinner in need of Your grace. I confess that I've been in control of my own life up to this point, and I've not done a good job. I recognize that I need You. I apologize for thinking that I could live without You.

But, now I come to You declaring that I believe that Jesus Christ is Lord and the son of God. I believe He took off His divinity in Heaven and came down to earth wrapped in flesh in order to live a perfect life as an example and an offering for Your people. I declare that I believe that Jesus was fully God and fully man all at the same time; and I believe that He died on the cross for me at Calvary to restore me to right relationship with You so that I could spend eternity worshipping You. And I believe that Jesus was raised from the dead on the third day.

God, I declare that, from this day forward, I surrender my life to You. I give You control of my life and I ask You to come into my heart and teach me to live for You. I thank You for the gift of Your presence through Your Holy Spirit that will live in me from this day forward. And, I thank You that Your Spirit will speak with me and teach me to live a life that honors You and points the world back to You. Thank You for coming to die for me so that I may live for You. Thank You for saving me! I pray this prayer in the mighty and matchless name of Jesus, Amen!

INDEX B
Scripture References

For select chapters, you will need the following lists of scriptures to complete the suggested activity.

Surrendering Rejection
Psalm 27:10
John 15:18-21
Isaiah 53:3
John 1:11
Luke 10:16
Psalm 118:22
Matt. 10:14

Surrendering My Mind
Galatians 5:17
Philippians 4:8-9
2 Corinthians 10:5

Psalm 103:8

Psalm 46:1

Romans 8:28

Philippians 4:19

1 Peter 5:7

John 1:12

John 3:16

Psalm 31:19

Psalm 84:11

Galatians 6:9

Psalm 55:22

Luke 12:6-7

Psalm 107:9

2 Peter 1:3

Isaiah 43:1

Romans 8:38-39

Jeremiah 29:11

Ezekiel 36:26

Isaiah 63:9

Find your own verses!!!

INDEX C –
Musical Playlist

This playlist can be found on Spotify, YouTube and Apple Music. Support these artists by heading over to the streaming platform of your choice and listening and even purchasing those that bless you!

IPoS Inspiration Playlist

- "Everything Changes" by Anthony Evans
- "Journal" by Casey J
- "Withholding Nothing" by William McDowell
- "Ask" by Anthony Evans
- "Cycles" by Jonathan McReynolds
- "A Heart That Forgives" by Kevin Levar
- "Thy Will" by Hilary Scott

ACKNOWLEDGEMENTS

To my siblings, **Joseph & Nicole, John & Renee, Charysse & AJ**: thank you for loving me as I am for all of these years; for supporting and encouraging me even when it seemed I had nothing to show for my obedience to God. To my parents, John Strothers, Claudine Mitchell, and step-mom, Deborah Jenkins: thank you for ALL of the sacrificial love you've given over the years. Thank you for sacrificing for me even when I didn't realize you were. Thank you for sacrificing so that your children could be better and do more than you ever prayed and dreamed. Thank you for years of prayers and love even when we were ungrateful. I love you all SO dearly, family!

To two of my three Best Sister-Friends, Sattarah and Tanika: thank you both for letting me be authentically me. Thank you for laughing with me, crying with me, trusting me, loving me, encouraging me, teaching me, letting me go on countless family vacations (Sattarah & my Bolden Family) and inviting me in to be a full-fledged member of your families. I think you know what it means to me that your parents and son call me daughter and godmommy, respectively (Sattarah); and that you and your sisters affectionately call me "Sister" (Tanika). I don't know that a woman could ask for better, more gifted, more genuine Sister-Friends and I'm grateful that God loves me so much that I didn't even have to ask, He just sent you to me. I love y'all!

To my spiritual family, My spiritual parents (Pops & D Washington), and all my spiritual coverings (Pastor B & Rev. D, Pastor Tookes) as well as my whole Macedonia Church of Pittsburgh Family: you all will probably never fully understand how much your love and support over these many years have helped me grow and develop into the woman that I am today and how they continue to spur me on to become God's original design of me. Needless to say, I can never repay you all for the years of love you have lavished on me. I am grateful for each and every one of you. I'm grateful for all that you've poured into me, not asking anything in return. Thank you for loving me as I am.

To all my "Little Sisters", Aaliyah, Adia, Alisha, Aniah, Chelsea, Jarah, Jordan, Lailonny, Lynette and Stephanie, Thank you for trusting me to pour into you. I pray that this book inspires you to keep pursuing surrender in your own lives until you've surrendered ALL of you! I love you!

To my AMAZING team of Advanced (BETA) Readers, Monique Bivins, Karen Merritt, Sattarah Bolden, Tanika Harris, Adia Hearns, Aaliyah Jones, Emiola Oriola and Owen Weston: the words 'thank you' don't even begin to scratch the surface of my gratitude to you all for your time, your effort, your energy and your honest, loving feedback. You cannot even fully know how much your partnership with me in this process means. Even your feedback was confirmation of God's word to me. Thank you all so very much!

To my editor, Ms. Theresa Edwards, I never had the privilege of having you as an English teacher in your years of teaching, but if I had, you would have easily been my favorite teacher of all time. Thank you for graciously agreeing to pour through the right-brained ramblings of a "squirrel chasing"(going off on tangents) woman just trying to be obedient to God. Like, seriously, I go on so many tangents… I digress. (LOL. Inside joke) In all fairness, I think it's only right to point out that I didn't take EVERY piece of advice she offered, so when you see that there are contractions out the wazoo and a phrase that ends in a preposition, it's NOT Ms. Theresa's fault. I made some very intentional language choices in this book.

Ms. Theresa, I was so encouraged by our communications and your notes throughout the editing process. I dare say I will NEVER have another editor whom I treasure as much as you. I will always keep this manuscript safe and close to my heart, if for no other reason than to revisit the life-affirming notes that you left in the margins of this manuscript… in the margins of my heart. I will treasure every phone conversation in which you shared your wisdom and love. Thank you so very much for your selfless investment in partnering with me in this process. I am ever grateful to God for you, Ms. Theresa!

Finally, to my accountability partner, my Rafiki, Amylicious: There is not another person on this planet that could be to me who, and what you are. You don't just accept me as I am, you give me permission to be who God created me to be. And although I shouldn't need permission, you never judge me in those moments when I do; you just graciously and lovingly tell me it's okay.

Thank you for talking me off of so many ledges and cliffs, no matter how high, steep or treacherous. There were moments when you understood that words would not bring me back from the brink, only the silent reassurance of your presence that pointed to God's ever-presence would do it; so you silently stood and held my hand and let me cry on your shoulder. Thank you for getting me." Thank you for pulling my card when I get out of pocket, for always pointing me back to Jesus and for inviting me into your family as one of your own. You are my Sister, my Accountability Partner, my "Pull Down" Partner, and my Rafiki (Friend). I love you more dearly than you'll ever know.

ABOUT THE AUTHOR

Angelique Antoinette Strothers (pronounced: ON-juh-leek, ON-twuh-net, STRUH-thers) is a native of Pittsburgh, Pennsylvania. She is currently on the worship staff at Macedonia Church of Pittsburgh where she's been a faithfully committed servant-leader for more than fourteen years. She is a consummate creative who communicates The Gospel of Jesus Christ through every medium at her disposal. Angelique is an anointed psalmist, through whom God penetrates atmospheres, breaks yokes and delivers. She is a skilled and prolific writer of prose, poetry, stage plays and music as well as an engaging speaker and gifted actress.

There are two constants that are evident in all that Angelique does, her love for God and her incessant sense of humor — she is a firm believer that the abundant life God offers includes a well-developed funny bone and laugh lines. Whether she is leading worship, speaking, acting or writing, you will always find God at the center; and because God remains her priority, He has opened many doors for her to use her gifts to do what she loves.

Angelique has been invited to lead worship and speak all over the city of Pittsburgh and across the United States. She has been privileged to act in productions across Pennsylvania and the surrounding areas; she has also written many celebrated stage plays, poems and songs. As Angelique remains faithful and submitted to God, He continues to increase her gifts and platform.

While Angelique is grateful and honored to serve God on every platform He provides, at her core, she remains His humble daughter who lives to make His name famous in all the earth. She understands that Kingdom advancement happens when the people of God understand their purpose and identity in God, and walk fully in that calling. Angelique believes and applies the Word of God found in 2 Peter 1:10 "My brothers and sisters, God called you and chose you to be His. Do your best to live in a way that shows you really are God's called and chosen people. If you do all this, you will never fall." (ERV)

Stay connected:
www.pursuingsurrender.com
FB & IG: @pursuingsurrenderllc

"Your freedom

will only come through your

surrender to God."

~Angelique Strothers

Made in the USA
Middletown, DE
09 April 2022